Razama-Snaz!

A Listener's Guide to Nazareth

ROBERT LAWSON

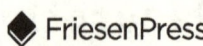 FriesenPress

Suite 300 - 990 Fort St
Victoria, BC, V8V 3K2
Canada

www.friesenpress.com

Copyright © 2016 by Robert Lawson

First Edition — 2016

All rights reserved.

No part of this publication may be reproduced in any form, or by any means, electronic or mechanical, including photocopying, recording, or any information browsing, storage, or retrieval system, without permission in writing from FriesenPress.

ISBN

978-1-4602-8638-8 (Hardcover)
978-1-4602-8639-5 (Paperback)
978-1-4602-8640-1 (eBook)

1. MUSIC, GENRES & STYLES, ROCK

Distributed to the trade by The Ingram Book Company

Table of Contents

1	Introduction	1961–1968
5	Nazareth	1971
11	Exercises	1972
15	Razamanaz	1973
21	Loud 'n' Proud	1973
27	Rampant	1974
33	Hair of the Dog	1975
43	Dan McCafferty	1975
49	Close Enough For Rock 'n' Roll	1976
55	Play 'n' the Game	1976
61	Expect No Mercy	1977
69	No Mean City	1979
75	Malice In Wonderland	1980
85	The Fool Circle	1981

91	Snaz	1981
101	2XS	1983
109	Sound Elixir	1983
115	The Catch	1984–1985
123	Cinema	1986–88
127	Into the Ring	1986
133	Snakes 'n' Ladders	1989
139	No Jive	1991
151	Move Me	1994
157	Boogaloo	1998–2001
163	Homecoming	2002–2007
177	The Newz	2008
183	Big Dogz/The Naz Box	2010–2013
191	Rock 'n' Roll Telephone	2014
203	Manny Charlton	1990–2015
211	Carl Sentence and No Means Of Escape	2015

For my father, Dennis Lawson, for inspiring a lifelong love of music and a burning desire to figure out why it matters so damned much.

Acknowledgements

First of all, my greatest thanks have to go to the original architects of the Nazareth legacy, who started me down this path so many decades ago. A sincere thank you to Dan McCafferty, Manny Charlton, Pete Agnew, and Darrel Sweet. Thanks also to Zal Cleminson, Billy Rankin, and everyone else who has stood proudly under the Nazareth banner. The music you created made a strong impression on my childhood, and it has not abated one bit since.

I have nothing but appreciation for the team of Nazareth experts who contributed to this project. They are: early supporter Richard Kolke, mega-contributor Nick Koster, all-around good guy Jon Hahn, angel of positive reinforcement Kandice Abbott, great mate Ian Naismyth, the main man Joe Geesin (www.JoeGeesin.com), the ever helpful Michael Tasker, new friend Dimitry E. Epstein (www.dmme.net), the incredibly knowledgeable Roni Ramos Amorin (http://roninazareth.blogspot.com.br/), Airton Silva, Helge Rognstad (www.fluffyjackets.co.uk), plus everyone who contributed fan memories to the text. (You'll find those generous souls credited elsewhere within.) If any of you wonderful people are ever anywhere close to the city of Toronto, drinks are on me.

Special gratitude to my pal Martin Popoff for support and encouragement throughout the project. Martin's books about Thin Lizzy, Deep Purple, Dio, and Rainbow are all essential reading for hard rock fans and are highly recommended. Please check him out at www.martinpopoff.com. I'm just thankful he never got around to doing one about Nazareth!

Other friends whose writings have inspired and influenced me over the years include Dave Bidini, Holly Cara Price, Hank Davis, Errol Nazareth, Aaron Lupton, Sean Kelly, Allan Tong, Monika Warzecha, and Laura Stanley.

A heartfelt cheer to the many mates of mine with whom I have spent numerous hours over the years enjoying conversation (and pints) about music, movies, and pop culture. There is always something new to learn when your crew of esteemed lads includes Frank Brasil, Vince Oliver, Gord Koch, Jim Hansen, Rick Brasil, Duart Silva, Mark Trump, Graham Haggart, Andrew Meredith, Chris Drossos, Paul Wood, Joe Gallant, Scott Verge, Justin Chasty, Jeff Enchin, Sean Passmore, Bret Boyd, and, of course, Nick Vasev. Solidarity forever!

Love to my dear daughter, Nina Lawson, whose very existence has made me a better person—plus, we get to go to rock concerts (and baseball games) together. Someday, I hope to take you to a Nazareth show.

Finally, never-ending hugs to my partner Vanessa Skembaris for sharing a passion for music and always being there. Things are better with you, babe! Believe that.

As for me, after a year and a half of listening to practically nothing but Nazareth (Sunday mornings were reserved for recordings on the Impulse jazz label), I'm ready to take a break from obsessing over a single band from the 1970s.

Now, where did I leave those Blue Oyster Cult records . . . ?

Prologue

Growing up in the late 1970s/early 1980s, a big part of my hard rock musical diet was made up of AC/DC, Aerosmith, Cheap Trick, Kiss, and Van Halen. (The important qualifier "early" applies to each of them, it must be said.)

However, special place in this roster of hard rock heroes was held by Scotland's own Nazareth. Something about the blend of Dan McCafferty's gritty vocals and the smooth slide guitar work from Manny Charlton was a winning combination to my young, impressionable ears.

My naive understanding of the band's relative place in rock lore is demonstrated best by the following incident. On December. 9, 1982, the band played Maple Leaf Gardens in Toronto in between openers Rose Tattoo and the unfortunately ill-fated and under-appreciated Mk II Aerosmith featuring Jimmy Crespo headlining. Full disclosure: Your author was attending high school at the time of this concert and, upon overhearing a fellow student talking about the Aerosmith/Nazareth show they had seen the night, asked, "Which band was the headliner?" Such was my overestimation of Nazareth's career compared to Aerosmith, yet I stand by this assessment today.

An opportunity to scoop up a handful of albums from a local used record store in 1987 added to a collection that already featured well-worn copies of *Razamanaz*, *Hair of the Dog*, and, of course, *Snaz*, one of my top ten live albums of all time. After that, I kept buying Nazareth albums with varying degrees of enjoyment. Some releases were better than others, but there was never a time when I thought the group should not have entered the recording studio. In fact, Billy Rankin's celebrated early 1990s return to the band had an invigorating impact, and his replacement, Jimmy Murrison, has brought his own distinctive six-string firepower.

With the 2014 retirement of frontman Dan McCafferty, the group seemed in jeopardy of collapse, but sole original member, bassist Pete Agnew, continues to rail against this perhaps inevitable conclusion, leading the band with regular, well-received touring.

A note regarding individual album info: When the title of each album is first mentioned in regards to its original release date, the album's specific product code is written in parentheses. Original singles, promotional releases, international editions, and even bootlegs also include this information, if available. While not everyone will care about this, I present it for the collector who might need the differential info on say, the *Rampant* album (i.e., CREST 15, TOPS 106, and even SAH 134). Hopefully this is not too intrusive for those able to lead a fulfilling life without the need for such information.

I envy you.

Introduction
1961–1968

The genesis of Nazareth took place back in 1961 in Dunfermline, Scotland, where local pop music cover band the Shadettes gigged regularly with a brighter future ahead. Among their early lineups were the future Nazareth rhythm section of bassist Pete Agnew and drummer Darrell Sweet. In early 1965, Dan McCafferty joined as lead vocalist, having no previous experience, which apparently meant less than the fact he had been a close friend of Agnew's since the tender age of five.

The band continued playing recent chart hits during residencies at local venues like the Kinema Ballroom and the Belleville Hotel until late 1968, when guitarist Manny Charlton came on board, having played previously in contemporaries the Mark V and the Red Hawks. With the Mark V, Charlton had recorded a single in 1964 called "Baby What's Wrong" or "Tango" (TF 513) for the Fontana label, while in 1966 the Red Hawks released a single written by Charlton called "Friday Night" (595001) with the B-side "Lonely Boy" on LP Records.

At the time, a strong circuit of bars and clubs in Scotland helped fledging bands get regular work, and the Shadettes made the most of the opportunity. In Edinburgh, they played the Place and the Top Story. In Glasgow, it was the Picasso, Locarno, and Electric Garden, while in Aberdeen, the guys performed at the Beach Ballroom.

Having to learn a minimum of three new chart toppers each week reflected the band's hard-working ethic. Their ability to add personality to these covers would pay off handsomely in later years, where numerous cover songs became ingrained in the public's conscience as Nazareth classics.

Among the covers of lightweight pop songs, the band started adding material into which they could actually sink their creative teeth. Chuck Berry and Otis Redding songs were introduced, followed by heavier material from groups like Deep Purple and Led Zeppelin.

The lads were content with this arrangement while balancing decent day jobs and family responsibilities. Then, in December 1968, everything changed, with the name of the group switching to the mysterious and slightly forbidding Nazareth (taken from the 1968 song "The Weight" by the Band) and a serious drive to compose quality original material. Soon, they quite their day jobs and relocated to London, where manager Bill Fehilly, who had amassed a small fortune running bingo halls, worked to secure them a record deal, eventually securing the boys a contract with Pegasus Records, an offshoot of B&C Records.

While gigging regularly as the opening act for international artists like the Who, Cream, Deep Purple, Rory Gallagher, and Atomic Rooster, Nazareth honed their chops and prepared to enter a proper recording studio.

The real adventure was about to begin.

Nazareth
1971

BACKGROUND

The late 1971 release of Nazareth's eponymous debut album *Nazareth* (PEG 10) kick-started a forty-year career of hard rock excellence, even if that initial volley was not exactly in the heavy vein for which they would soon become well known.

Although intimidated by the size of their first visit to a professional recording facility (Trident Studios in London, only guitarist Manny Charlton had any experience in such a setting), the band was more than comfortable with the material to be captured on tape. They were so comfortable, in fact, that the sessions were completed within three weeks under the watch of producer David Hitchcock and engineer Roy Thomas Baker.

ALBUM OVERVIEW

The album opens confidently with "Witchdoctor Woman," which is filled with dirty guitars and shrieking lead vocals. Next up is "Dear John," featuring suitably honky-tonk piano courtesy of sessions player Pete Wingfield, clearly the star of the track. Following that is

"Empty Arms, Empty Heart," an over-driven slice of proto-psychedelic guitar rock with some prog elements.

On "I Had A Dream," bassist Pete Agnew provides a gentle, yearning lead vocal over delicate acoustic guitar strumming. This appearance on lead vocals isn't as surprising as it may seem, as Agnew was the guitarist/lead vocalist in the Shadettes for a few years before McCafferty joined. His voice is fine on a mellow track like "I Had A Dream," but in the future, Agnew wisely stuck to harmony vocals as the band explored heavier material.

"Red Light Lady" shows off a surprisingly ambitious side to such an inexperienced group of musicians. The first half of the song chugs along fine in the bluesy rock vein of most of the album, but the last half has a full orchestral accompaniment.

McCafferty drops his voice down to an even deeper and darker growl for the choruses on the thudding track "Fat Man."

Somewhat similar to "I Had A Dream," "Country Girl" is an example of the more introspective side of the band's songwriting style at the time. Charlton adds some authentic steel guitar to compliment the track.

The lone cover on the album is "Morning Dew," written by Canadian folk singer Bonnie Dobson, a tune that was a regular part of their set back when they were playing only other peoples' material (in this case, probably learned from the version that appeared on the Jeff Beck Group's 1968 debut album). The rhythm section creates a radiating tension, with occasional blasts from Charlton's piercing guitar, while McCafferty takes his time before digging in full force.

The album ends with "The King Is Dead," a dark ballad given dramatic flourish with the use, once again, of a classical orchestra.

RELEASE AND RECEPTION

The record met with a lukewarm reaction. Debut UK single "Dear John" (PGS 2), paired with the non-album track "Friends," failed to garner much interest, but the label thought enough of it to re-release it using their new "PEG" purple label (but still assigned PGS 2), still with little success. It probably didn't help that the B-side "Friends" was inexplicably retitled as the unintentionally prophetic "Occasional Failure."

The "Dear John/Friends" pairing was also released in Germany. A mono release of "Dear John" (6073 220 on Philips) with "Fat Man" on the flip-side did chart in in France.

The follow-up single, "Morning Dew" (PGS 4), paired with the hard-driving non-album track "Spinning Top," was released only in Germany and charted similarly. Not only should "Spinning Top" have been considered for the album, its guitar solo has Charlton channeling his inner-Ritchie Blackmore to great effect. A promotional single for "Morning Dew" was released in the US, featuring both mono and stereo mixes of the song.

After releasing the album, the band went back to what they knew best: gigging and writing new material for the follow-up. Unfortunately, a seven-date UK jaunt opening for Black Sabbath on their *Master Of Reality* tour was cancelled when three of the four members of Sabbath got sick.

On September 21, 1971, the band played the Marquee Club in London as the opening act for Keef Hartley, a gig that was captured on tape. This low-fi recording conveys all of the clamour and clatter of an early, sweat-drenched gig. Murky sound quality aside, the recording is an historically important document of the band's lean years. Darrell Sweet in particular plays with more enthusiasm and fire than usually heard on record. His drums knock out a tribal rhythm to introduce the Allman Brothers' "Black Hearted Woman" before Manny Charlton unleashes a volley of power chords. Next is "The Wrong Time," originally by Spooky Tooth (from their 1970 album *The Last Puff*), featuring a fascinating, hypnotic guitar part.

A trio of tracks from the recently-released debut album follow. "Fat Man" has a thick, lumbering groove without the extra vocal effect heard on the album. Dan introduces the single "Dear John," saying, "We also wrote this one," and at the end of the song seems genuinely surprised by the crowd's positive reaction. "Empty Heart, Empty Arms" is given a raw delivery with a somewhat spacey middle section over which Charlton solos. "Take Me In Your Arms" is a Holland-Dozier-Holland-written Motown song that hit number twenty-two on the R&B chart in March 1968 when released by the Isley Brothers. In 1975, the Doobie Brothers (featuring future Nazareth producer Jeff "Skunk" Baxter) took the song to number eleven on the US charts. Dan introduces the track by saying, "This is an old soul number, which we've changed a wee bit."

"Appears Strange To Me" begins with Agnew's funky bass, over which Charlton layers chimes of guitar notes before McCafferty jumps in.

Another album track, "Morning Dew," begins with a long intro of ear-splitting feedback bursts from Charlton before the band hits its stride. Finally, "Witchdoctor Woman" has Dan shrieking while guitars and drums fight to fill any remaining spaces untarnished by the pounding din being birthed. The track ends with an extended solo from Charlton and then a loose jam to wind things up.

RE-ISSUES, RE-MASTERS, AND RE-RECORDINGS

In 1999, Castle Music reissued *Nazareth* on CD with five bonus tracks. The B-sides "Friends" and "Spinning Top," both sourced from vinyl copies, were excellent supplements to the record. Additionally, alternate edits exist of "Dear John," "Morning Dew," and "Friends." These "alternate edits" are fake versions created by reissue supervisor Robert Corich to add more bonus material.

The Eagle Records CD reissue has the bonus tracks "Dear John" (single edit), "Friends" (B-side), "Morning Dew" (alternate edit), "Friends" (alternate edit), "Morning Dew" (extended single version), and "Witchdoctor Woman" (alternate edit).

Nazareth was re-mastered again in 2009 by Salvo Music and paired on a single CD with their second album, *Exercises*, therefore, omitting all five bonus tracks. In the case of the fake "alternate edits," this is not a loss at all. In addition, this Salvo release incorrectly states that the original album was issued in January 1971.

Exercises
1972

BACKGROUND

After the disappointing reception to their debut album, Nazareth went back to Trident Studios in London to record the follow-up. *Nazareth* engineer Roy Thomas Baker returned as well, this time handling full production duties.

When released in June of 1972, *Exercises* (PEG 14) presented ten new original compositions touching various genres, including folk, country, and soft rock with nary a hard rock song in sight.

ALBUM OVERVIEW

Opening track "I Will Not Be Led" has Dan fronting a lush orchestra before the band kicks in with some much-needed muscle and funky bass. "Cat's Eye, Apple Pie" is a buoyant slice of playful country, no doubt inspired by Bob Dylan's *Nashville Skyline* album. It allows Charlton to indulge in some tasty acoustic picking, which shows another side of the versatile guitarist.

"In My Time" is a mellow lament in waltz time(!) saved by a stinging fuzz guitar solo. Finally, the propulsive boogie beat to "Woke Up This Morning" changes things up a bit. The tune ends with a noisy clash of guitars and then goes right into the mostly acoustic "Called Her Name."

"Fool About You" is another mostly acoustic number, while "Love Now You're Gone" has an odd, primitive synthesizer throughout. The next two songs, "Madeline" and "Sad Song," are both ballads, the former of which features an orchestra.

The album ends with a dramatic retelling of a legendary event in Scottish history, the February 12, 1692 mass killing of unsuspecting members of Clan MacDonald by forces representing Clan Campbell. "1692 (Glen Coe Massacre)" is complete with bagpipes, strings, and marching drums. (Darrell Sweet played in a drum corps as a lad.)

RELEASE AND RECEPTION

After the record was released, performing even worse chart-wise than its predecessor, the band put out a non-album single, "If You See My Baby" (PGS 5). Charlton rips a nicely distorted guitar solo on the stomping, glam rock-style track. The B-side, "Hard Living," foreshadows the heavier direction Nazareth would be favouring soon. The "If You See My Baby/Hard Living" pairing was also released in France.

On June 8, 1972, the band appeared on BBC Radio 1 with a live show recorded at the Paris Theatre in London. *Exercise* tracks, such as "Called Her Name" and "Fool About You," were played with extra enthusiasm not heard on the record, while an almost ten-minute cover of the Allman Brothers' "Black Hearted Woman" was given a groovy, low-slung reading. Charlton's second guitar solo during this tune quotes the famous Scottish standard "The Bonnie Banks o' Loch Lomond." These performances surfaced years later on the 1991 CD BBC *Radio 1 Live In Concert* and the 2001 double-CD archival set *Back To The Trenches: Live 1972–1984*, where they are erroneously reported to have been recorded in Canada in 1972.

On June 25, Nazareth played the Greyhound Pub in Fullham, London, a popular Scottish pub that hosted many bands over the years. Their set was comprised of songs that would be retired in the coming years, such as "Spinning Top," "Red Light Lady," "Fool About You," and "Dear John." They also did "Black Hearted Woman" and a cover of Chuck Berry's "Sweet Little Rock 'n' Roller."

Once again, the record was not successful upon release, so the band left to tour as the opening act for Deep Purple. This association was about to change the trajectory of their career forever.

RE-ISSUES, RE-MASTERS, AND RE-RECORDINGS

The album saw a 1975 release in Japan under the title *Exercise* (BT-5041). The sleeve features a cover photo of the band live on stage at the Rainbow Theatre opening for Deep Purple. (The same image was used years later for a bootleg CD of the June 25, 1972 Fullham, London show titled *Live In Greyhound 1972*.) *Exercise* was also released in the US as SP-3168.

The 1999 Castle CD re-master includes the non-album single "If You See My Baby" (listed incorrectly as a B-side) and it's flip, "Hard Living" plus an alternate edit of "1692 (Glencoe Massacre)." The version of "Hard Living" is listed as an alternate edit, which means two lines of lyrics have been removed to create a unique "new" version that did not exist originally.

In 2002, Eagle Records released their version of the album with the bonus tracks "If You See My Baby" and fake alternate edits of "Woke Up This Morning," "Love Now You're Gone," and "1962 (Glencoe Massacre)."

The 2009 Salvo reissue paired with the debut album has no supplemental material.

Razamanaz
1973

BACKGROUND

Touring as the opening act on Deep Purple's American and UK *Machine Head* and *Who Do We Think We Are* jaunts did more than just present the band to larger audiences.

After a particularly memorable show on February 27, 1973, in Newcastle, the band retired to the bar of the Gosforth Park Hotel, where they were staying. Deep Purple bassist Roger Glover joined the guys for drinks, and by the end of the evening, offered his services as producer. Glover's work on the 1972 self-titled album debut album by Ronnie James Dio's early band Elf was well known to Nazareth, being voracious music fans as well as performers.

The band felt the impact of having a relatively seasoned veteran in their corner immediately in two areas. First, feeling that the band's inexperience in the studio had led to somewhat stiff performances,

Glover arranged for the album to be recorded in the familiar surroundings of their rehearsal space, the Gang Hut, in Jamestown, Scotland. Second, Glover (one of the principle songwriters in Deep Purple) worked with the guys on the compositions to ensure the material was structured as strongly as possible. Nazareth had been previewing some of the new songs on the Deep Purple tour, and Glover already had some ideas to help polish the work to achieve maximum results. When *Razamanaz* (CREST 1) was released in May 1973, the hard work paid off handsomely.

ALBUM OVERVIEW

The title track bursts out of the speakers with a pounding sense of purpose, not unlike Deep Purple's "Speed King." Over a thick Manny Charlton riff, Dan embraces his new role as sinister master of ceremonies. Next, a primitive tribal beat opens a simmering cover of Leon Russell's "Alcatraz." A cover of Woody Guthrie's "Vigilante Man" (via Ry Cooder's arrangement) begins with mournful slide guitar, leads to military drums, and eventually McCafferty goes into full-on screamer mode. A muscular re-recording of "Woke Up This Morning" from *Exercises,* featuring prominent bass playing, brings the song to its full potential. "Night Woman" has a great Bo Diddley beat and confident bass guitar ,paving the way for Charlton's heavily flanged guitar. "Bad Bad Boy" picks up the pace with a fun, up-tempo slide guitar, betraying the mischievous wink behind McCafferty's vocals, which turn to screams.

Speaking of screams, "Sold My Soul" is a mid-tempo lament notable for Dan's anguished howling, "I sold my soul! To the devil!" Unfortunately, this track is the only song on *Razamanaz* that the band never played live. "Too Bad Too Sad" is a quick, little rocker that sprints along with a Chuck Berry-styled guitar break early on. The album ends with "Broken Down Angel," welcoming the listener with an agreeably smooth guitar lick and catchy chorus. The proven harmonies of McCafferty and Agnew sound heavenly over a relentless, stomping beat. This is the only song not recorded in Scotland. Instead, Glover chose to lay it down at Island Studios in London.

Among the demos recorded for the album are rudimentary versions of "Broken Down Angel" (featuring some different riffing and a completely unique guitar solo), "Night Woman," "Vigilante Man," "Alcatraz," "Razamanaz," and "Bad Bad Boy." Also included is the new song "On The Run," an electric blues thump, less an actual song than an insistent vamp. "On The Run" did not make it to the final release.

17

RELEASE AND RECEPTION

Chart-wise, the album hit number one hundred and fifty-seven in the US (SP-4396), the band's first American placement on the sales charts, number forty-eight in Germany, number thirty-nine in Canada (where it received platinum certification), and its highest placement, number eleven in the UK.

"Broken Down Angel" was released as a single (MOON 1) with "Witchdoctor Woman" on the B-side and far surpassed any of the band's previous seven-inchers, charting at number nine in the UK, number twenty in Ireland, and even hitting number fifty-seven in faraway Australia. It was also released in France, Spain, Italy, Greece, and South Africa. A version that had "Woke Up This Morning" on the flip was issued in Holland and Yugoslavia.

An A&M Records US promo-only single was released for "Broken Down Angel" (1453) that paired mono and stereo versions of the song. The second single from the album, "Bad Bad Boy" (MOON 9), also helped expand the group's reach, hitting number ten in the UK and number fifteen in Ireland. The UK "Bad Bad Boy" single had two B-sides on the flip: "Spinning Top," which was the B-side to the 1972 UK single "Morning Dew" (PGS 4) and "Hard Living," which was recycled from the B-side of the September 1972 non-album single "If You See My Baby" (PGS 5). A German single of "Bad Bad Boy" was paired with "Broken Down Angel," while the Yugoslavian version came with "Razamanaz" on the B-side. In the US, a promo single for the album's title track had the album version on one side and an edited version for radio play on the flip.

On July 22, the band appeared at the second Summer Rock Festival in Frankfurt, Germany along with Sly and the Family Stone, Rory Gallagher, and Rod Stewart and the Faces, among others.

Nazareth's brief set consisted of "Night Woman," "Razamanaz," "Alcatraz," "Vigilante Man" (with some hard pounding near the end), Joe Tex's "Goin' Down," "Morning Dew," and "Bad Bad Boy." Dan attempts to get a reaction out of the crowd before "Morning Dew," shouting, "You've been asleep long enough!"

RE-ISSUES, RE-MASTERS, AND RE-RECORDINGS

Razamanaz was issued on CD in the UK by Castle and includes four bonus tracks, the B-sides "Hard Living" and "Spinning Top, an alternate edit of "Woke Up This Morning," and "Witchdoctor Woman" from the band's self-titled debut album, which was used as a B-side to the "Broken Down Angel" single.

The thirtieth anniversary reissue from Eagle Records in Germany has three extra songs: "Hard Living," "Spinning Top," and an alternate edit of the title track. This "Razamanaz" alternate edit also appears on the 2004 two-CD compilation *Maximum XS*, the liner notes stating that it was "probably intended for single release," although according to former Nazareth press secretary Joe Geesin, the song "was never openly and commercially considered by the band as a single, although it did appear in promo form in the USA and as a B-side in Yugoslavia and the Philippines."

The 2009 *Salvo* CD has a total of six bonus tracks—the previously mentioned B-sides of "Hard Living" and "Spinning Top" plus four tracks from a BBC radio show featuring the band playing at Maidvale Studios. Broadcast on March 26, 1973, the songs performed are "Razamanaz" (featuring Charlton's extremely dry guitar), strong versions of "Night Woman" and "Broken Down Angel" and finally "Vigilante Man," which is missing the military drum part heard so prominently on the studio take.

Loud 'n' Proud
1973

BACKGROUND

The runaway success of *Razamanaz* meant immediate pressure from the record company for Nazareth to provide a follow up. Duplicating the methods seemed like a sure way to replicate the success, so the band and their producer, now ex-Deep Purple member Roger Glover, reconvened at the Gang Hut rehearsal studio in Jamestown and went to work.

In less than two weeks, the album was complete, and in November 1973, Nazareth's fourth album, *Loud 'n' Proud* (CREST 4), was released, preceded by the single "This Flight Tonight," which came out in October.

The record jacket's striking depiction of a braying peacock displaying its iridescent tail feathers conveyed the group's new sense of pride perfectly.

ALBUM OVERVIEW

Things kick off with "Go Down Fighting," a hefty chugger with spoken bridges and an almost hidden acoustic guitar deep in the mix.

The excellent "Not Fakin' It" has a distorted effect on McCafferty's vocals, as if he's calling in on a crackling, long-distance line. In the song, Dan compares his occupation to those of such historical figures as Billy the Kid, Jack the Ripper, Jesus, and Cleopatra, stating, "Me, I'm just a rock n roll singer!" At least he's keeping it real.

Bassist Pete Agnew's choice for a second single, "Turn On Your Receiver," is a musclebound rocker over a stomping glam beat.

Next, the group covers a song by one of their favourite bands, Little Feat. "Teenage Nervous Breakdown" appeared originally on Little Feat's 1972 album *Sailin' Shoes*. It's a pretty faithful rendition, just slightly heavier thanks to a rock-solid riff and no horn section.

"Free Wheeler" is a snappy, little sprinter with additional percussion provided by Glover and ends with a tasteful guitar solo.

Originally on Joni Mitchell's landmark album *Blue* (1971), Nazareth effectively transforms the gentle "This Flight Tonight" into a true barnstormer. A galloping rhythm is broken by slashing power chords and McCafferty snarling innocent lines like, "Hope you got your heat turned on, baby," with a threatening tone that adds an element of danger. Sounding like he is singing through a telephone line adds an interesting but unobtrusive effect to the song.

The final two tracks were not recorded at the Gang Hut rehearsal studio. Instead, they were laid down at Apple Studios in London.

"Child In The Sun" is a tender ballad with Pete Agnew handling lead vocals on the first verse, then later with an a capella finish.

"Ballad Of Hollis Brown" from Bob Dylan's 1964 album *The Times They Are A-Changin'* gets a complete overhaul even more radical than what was done to "This Flight Tonight." Dylan's original recording was a solo acoustic performance. Nazareth adds fuzz bass, a lumbering melody, wind sound effects, and a noisy sense of doom comparable to early Black Sabbath. The sludge is broken occasionally by McCafferty's unsettling shrieking.

RELEASE AND RECEPTION

The album improved upon the band's chart appearances thus far, hitting number one hundred and fifty in the US, number seventeen in Canada (SP-3609), earning them another platinum award, and number ten in the UK. "This Flight Tonight" was released as a single (MOON 14) with "Called Her Name" on the B-side and had decent traction, hitting number eleven on the UK charts, number one in Germany, and number two in Australia while also seeing release in Greece and Yugoslavia. A version with "Go Down Fighting" on the B-side was released in Spain, Mozambique, and Canada and hit number three in France. A US promo single featured mono and stereo mixes on each side.

To help promote the new release, Nazareth lip-synched "This Flight Tonight" on the German TV show *Disco '74*.

RE-ISSUES, RE-MASTERS, AND RE-RECORDINGS

The 1996 Castle CD adds three bonus tracks: the single of "This Flight Tonight," credited as the "US Version" (the difference in the mix being minimal, if at all), the cancelled second single "Go Down Fighting" (also called the "US version" and which is also virtually unchanged from the album cut), and the B-side to that cancelled single, "The Ballad Of Hollis Brown," which is actually an edited version (5:05 minutes vs. the album's 9:07 minutes) that fades out early to omit the last four (out of eleven) verses. The Castle CD states incorrectly that the album was released originally in early 1974.

The 2001 Eagle Records reissue repeats the three bonus tracks from the Castle disc and adds an edited version of the song "Free Wheeler," which is surely not authentic, as it was never considered for a single release.

The 2010 Salvo CD has four extra songs: "Turn On Your Receiver," "Too Bad Too Sad," "Razamanaz," and "Bad Bad Boy," all recorded live for the BBC on Aug 13, 1973, and none of which are on either the 1996 Castle or the 2001 Eagle Records issues. Of course, this recording is from before the album was even started, so three of the four songs were to promote the then current release *Razamanaz*. But it's cool to get an early listen to "Turn On Your Receiver," and the additional three tracks are all excellent, high-octane versions with gritty, in-your-face, lead vocals. Of the four, only "Razamanaz" is new, the others having appeared on the 1998 two-CD compilation *At The Beeb*.

In 1987, a Nazareth hits album *Hot Tracks* featured an extended version of "This Flight Tonight," which was not used on any of the three catalogue reissue editions. It's a good thing, too, as it adds the chorus after the second verse to make the song artificially longer, and the edit is far from seamless.

Fifteen years after *Loud 'n' Proud*, Heaven's Gate from Wolfsburg, Germany covered "This Flight Tonight" on their 1988 album *In Control*. This version is slightly sped up with giant drums and Ronnie James Dio-style vocals.

Ex-Hanoi Rocks frontman Michael Monroe covered the song "Not Fakin' It" on his 1989 solo album, which, in tribute to one of his favourite bands, was also titled *Not Fakin' It*. For their 1997 self-titled album, Iron Savior (from Hamburg, Germany) laid down a power metal version of "This Flight Tonight," which is perhaps more a tribute to Heaven's Gate than to Nazareth (never mind Joni Mitchell).

Rampant
1974

BACKGROUND

The relentless pace continued with the band quickly recording a new album in between extensive touring. Their first to be done outside of the UK, recording on *Rampant* began at the convention centre in Montreux, Switzerland, using the famed Rolling Stone Mobile Unit (both intimately familiar to producer Roger Glover) with vocals finished up at Ian Gillan's Kingsway Recorders studio in London.

Rampant (CREST 15) was released in May 1974 and was a valid successor to *Razamanaz* and *Loud 'n' Proud*, adding Americana influences more prominently than before. The result of heavy touring in the US also manifested itself in the lyrical content with tracks like "Jet Lag" and "Shanghai'd In Shanghai" detailing issues that could only befall a traveling rock band.

ALBUM OVERVIEW

The album kicks off strong with the fuzz guitar of "Silver Dollar Forger," a rowdy tune broken into two sections, the second being new for Nazareth, a spacey prog-rock instrumental.

"Glad When You're Gone" is a rowdy bit of Stones-style fun with soulful female backing vocals.

This is followed by "Loved And Lost," a bluesy, emotional, low-key piece that begins with haunting opening verses. Eventually, the heartbreak overload nudges this one into total despair.

Next up is the single from the album, "Shanghai'd In Shanghai," a friendly basher with female backing vocals, a catchy chorus and, Deep Purple's Jon Lord on honky-tonk piano. A nice touch comes after the line "we've got a gig, second billing to the Rolling Stones!" when Charlton adds the classic "Satisfaction" riff.

"Jet Lag" is a mid-paced lament about life on the road with a talk-box guitar solo and even a joke. Dan tries to call home from the road, but when he tells the operator that he needs to reach Scotland, she can't understand his accent and asks, "Could you spell that for me again?"

On "Light My Way," a rumbling bass guitar, echo-laden vocals, and a spacey guitar solo take the listener on an interstellar journey. "Light My Way" is the only track on *Rampant* that the group has never played live.

"Sunshine" is a decent, mostly acoustic ballad that probably should have been issued as a second single.

The sole cover song on the record, the Yardbirds' 1966 single "Shapes Of Things," rises majestically with booming drums and McCafferty eliciting extreme terror with one of his most malevolent vocal performances.

"Shapes" ends with a one-minute instrumental coda of astral effects titled "Space Safari," flirting again with prog-rock tendencies. This also should have been considered as a single.

RELEASE AND RECEPTION

The album hit number thirteen on the UK charts, number one hundred and fifty-seven in the US (SP-3641), and number eighty in Canada, where it achieved gold certification. The single "Shanghai'd In Shanghai" paired with "Love, Now You're Gone" (MOON 22) failed to break the Top Forty in the UK, but it fared more favourably in Austria (number seven) and Switzerland, where it peaked at number four. It also saw release in France, Japan, and South Africa. A release with "Cat's Eye Apple Pie" as the B-side was put out in Germany, where it reached number fourteen on the charts. In Spain, "Shanghai'd In Shanghai" was paired with "Sunshine" for single release. "Glad When You're Gone" with "Light My Way" on the B-side appeared as a single in Holland.

On May 16, the band played at Sheffield City Hall, where longtime British fan Phil Atkin saw them. "They opened with 'Silver Dollar Forger' but with the instrumental outro first," he recalls. "Manny came in with the riff about three minutes in. The Sheffield crowd didn't appreciate the 'dullness' of this and got shirty but improved. I thought it was ace. 'Shapes Of Things' was great. They played all the singles, and it was pre-*Hair of the Dog*, so the bagpipes were for 'Jet Lag.' They did all the post-'Broken Down Angel' singles, 'Razamanaz,' 'Vigilante Man,'

'Teenage Nervous Breakdown,' and then closed the show with 'Woke Up This Morning.' Lyrics to 'Bad Bad Boy' were changed from 'old town girl' to 'Sheffield girl,' the way to a crowd's heart!"

Nazareth also played the prestigious Pinkpop Festival in the Netherlands, where Pete Agnew wore an A&M Records T-shirt, reflecting the band's American label.

From June 7 to August 3, Nazareth played a nineteen-date US tour (including a stop in Vancouver) with headliners Blue Oyster Cult, who were promoting their significant *Secret Treaties* album. On June 21 in Buffalo, Golden Earing were added to the bill, while on June 25, Lynyrd Skynyrd joined the show in Greenville, and Brownsville Station was added for the June 28 show in Charlotte. For the July 6 show in Chattanooga, Rare Earth performed between sets by Nazareth and BOC. The last five dates of the tour also had opening act Kiss on the bill, whose self-titled debut album had just been released.

On August 10, the band appeared at the Turku Music Festival in Finland along with Strawbs and Procol Harum. An audience recording of the August 12 concert at Grona Lund in Stockholm, Sweden chronicles this pivotal period in the band's live history. During the fifteen-song set, Nazareth perform an incredible six tracks from the new album. Along with opener "Silver Dollar Forger," "Glad When You're Gone" (featuring stellar playing from Darrell Sweet), "Loved And Lost" (with a slow burn guitar solo), a lengthy "Jet Lag" (which ends with some bluesy jamming), "Shanghai'd In Shanghai," and "Shapes Of Things" are all presented, to the listeners' delight. Dan's introducing "a song which we've never recorded" is interesting knowing that the band would, in fact, record the Randy Newman cut "Guilty" for their next studio album, *Hair of the Dog*, although the audience had no way of knowing that at the time. The show ends with a rare cover of "Riot In Cell Block number 9," a number one hit single for the Robins in 1954.

RE-ISSUES, RE-MASTERS, AND RE-RECORDINGS

The re-mastered 1997 Castle CD featured three bonus tracks, the US single "Shanghai'd In Shanghai" (no different from the album cut), the B-side "Cat's Eye, Apple Pie," originally from the 1972 album *Exercises*, and a fake single edit to "Shapes Of Things" which removes most of the middle instrumental guitar-drums duel and then fades before the "Space Safari" coda.

The Eagle Records reissue includes those extra songs (omitting "Cat's Eye, Apple Pie") plus edited versions of "Silver Dollar Forger" (fades after last verse, removing part two completely) and "Sunshine" (juggles the first and second verses and removes the third).

In 2010, Salvo Records released a problematic new CD. Sound-wise, the disc is fantastic, but in terms of additional material, it is in trouble. The first bonus cut is "Down," which, considering it was the B-side to "Love Hurts," doesn't belong on *Rampant* at all. It should be on the reissue of 1975's *Hair of the Dog,* where it's flip side appears. The next seven tracks are BBC recordings from May 17, 1973 from the Golders Green Hippodrome. While these live, bass-heavy workouts are excellent, they really have nothing to do with the *Rampant* album and belong chronologically on a *Razamanaz* release, since they were laid down to promote that album. A DJ host even mentions after the first song that they are there to push the *Razamanaz* record!

Was there difficulty finding actual bonus material from the *Rampant* era? The 1998 double-CD set *At The Beeb* has four songs from that period, played live on April 8, 1974: "Shapes Of Things," "Silver Dollar Forger," "Glad You're Gone," and "Jet Lag." The problem with these tracks is that they are not live recordings made for the BBC but simply the studio versions found on the original *Rampant* album. These studio takes are mistakenly included on the live *At The Beeb* set in a textbook example of record company carelessness.

"Miss Misery" has a lurching, early Black Sabbath feel, a well-positioned slide solo, and picks up the pace near the end in a mad dash to the finish line.

The first cover song on the album is Randy Newman's "Guilty" from his 1974 album *Good Old Boys*, a sparse and bluesy ballad with Max Middleton of the Jeff Beck Group on piano.

The band switches back to the lumbering groove of "Changin' Times" with some unsettling McCafferty howling but eases up for a melodic guitar solo during the coda.

"Beggar's Day" originally appeared on the 1971 self-titled debut album by Crazy Horse sung by its writer, Nils Lofgren. Nazareth takes the menacing feel of the original and raises the stakes appropriately by digging even deeper into the swaggering beat and adding a Dan McCafferty vocal that could strip paint. "Beggar's Day" ends with an instrumental composition "Rose In The Heather," a sub-three minute coda that sounds not unlike "Country Girl" from the group's debut album. The "Rose In The Heather" ending is the only music from *Hair of the Dog* the band has never performed live.

"Whiskey Drinkin' Woman" has a southern-fried, percolating rhythm with a surprisingly clean lead vocal from McCafferty.

The primitive synthesizers on "Please Don't Judas Me" throb under acoustic guitar strumming and martial drums.

RELEASE AND RECEPTION

When presented with the album tapes, Jerry Moss, president of the band's North American label, A&M Records, chose wisely to swap out the Randy Newman cover "Guilty" with a track Nazareth did not even consider as an album cut. This move led to a massive change in the group's fortunes.

The song Moss chose, "Love Hurts," was an aching ballad recorded originally in 1960 by the Everly Brothers on their *A Date With The Everly Brothers* album but not released as a single. Roy Orbison was the first artist to have success with the song, hitting number five on the

Australian charts in 1961. No doubt, Nazareth was more familiar with the beautiful cover version by Gram Parsons with Emmylou Harris on his posthumous 1974 album *Grievous Angel*.

Added to the North American *Hair of the Dog* edition (SP-4511), "Love Hurts" was a massive hit and pushed the album to over two million sales in the United States alone. Issued as a non-album single everywhere else in the world led to similar success. The single "Love Hurts" (MOON 37), with the non-album B-side track "Down," hit the number one spot in Belgium, Canada, the Netherlands, Norway, and South Africa. It was a top ten hit in Australia, Denmark, New Zealand, and Sweden. It also reached number eleven in Austria and number fifteen in the UK. "Love Hurts" with "Down" on the B-side was also released as a single in Germany, France, Italy, Portugal, and Mexico. A version with "Hair of the Dog" as the B-side was released in Guatemala and the US, where it was a top ten hit. A German reissue switched the B-side to "This Flight Tonight." An Argentinian release had "My White Bicycle" as the flipside, and a version from the Philippines, interestingly, used "Razamanaz" as the second track.

The B-side "Down" is a great boogie rocker with handclaps, Pete Agnew's bass prominent in the mix, a muffled drum sound, and a near-falsetto lead vocal from McCafferty. Later, in November 1975, ex-Traffic drummer Jim Capaldi had a number four UK hit with a quite different version of "Love Hurts." Capaldi's version has a buoyant almost disco beat behind it but an excellent lead vocal, even if it is quite different from Dan's take.

The title track, "Hair of the Dog," was released as a single with "Too Bad Too Sad" as the B-side in the UK and as a promo single in the US. It was also paired with "Sunshine" for a German release and "Guilty" in Japan. "Guilty" received its own seven-inch release in South Africa with "Night Woman" on the B-side.

Hair of the Dog was the group's greatest chart success thus far, reaching number seventeen in the US, earning platinum certification, and number twenty in Canada, which was good enough for a gold record. The album was also released in Taiwan (JS-5061) with the text "Includes the hit single 'Love Hurts'" and in South Africa (6370 406) with "Featuring their hit single 'Love Hurts'" emblazoned proudly on the front cover sleeve.

The band made an appearance in June 1975 on the Austrian TV show *Spotlight* to promote the album by lip-synching four songs. "Miss Misery" has Charlton riffing on a black Gibson Les Paul, then taking a slide solo on a Fender Stratocaster mounted on a stand near the side of the stage. During "Hair of the Dog," McCafferty does his usual talk-box effect to Manny's guitar but without the bagpipes prop, which makes for a visual change. "This Flight Tonight" and "Love Hurts" were also "performed" during this appearance. They also lip-synched "Love Hurts" on the Dutch TV programme *Top Pop* and the German TV show *Musikladen*.

In 1975, the band signed a new record deal with Mountain Records, which promptly reissued their back catalogue, including re-releases of *Nazareth* (TOPC 5001), *Exercises* (TOPS 103), *Razamanaz* (TOPS 104), *Loud 'n' Proud* (TOPS 105), *Rampant* (TOPS 106), and *Hair of the Dog* (TOPS 107).

A month after the American release of *Hair of the Dog*, the band issued a non-album single, "My White Bicycle" (MOON 47), with the album cut "Miss Misery" on the B-side in the UK and France. A German pressing used "Too Bad Too Sad" as the flipside, while a US promo seven-inch repeated "My White Bicycle" on both sides.

"My White Bicycle" was recorded originally in 1967 by British psychedelic group Tomorrow featuring a pre-Yes Steve Howe on guitar. The Nazareth version is a happy, little burst of bubblegum pop. In October 1975, they released a single featuring two non-album tracks "Holy Roller" and "Railroad Boy" (TOP 3) in the UK, Germany, France, Portugal, Spain, and Australia. The picture sleeve for this release is a brilliant live shot of the band in concert with Pete Agnew brandishing a white Telecaster guitar.

"Holy Roller" is an upbeat, anti-evangelist rant, while the B-side "Railroad Boy," has dark, funky fuzz guitars and really should have been on the album. Pushing the latest single, the band lip-synched "Holy Roller" on the British TV show *Supersonic*. Both "My White Bicycle" and "Holy Roller" appeared on the group's first compilation record

Greatest Hits (TOPS 108), which was issued in November of that year. It also included four tracks from *Razamanaz* and two each from *Loud 'n' Proud*, *Rampant*, and *Hair of the Dog*. This excellent collection reached number one in Canada, earning platinum certification, and number fifty-four in the UK.

Throughout August and September of that year, Nazareth played a seven-date Canadian tour with opening act Rush, then promoting their third album *Caress Of Steel*. Longtime fan Richard Kolke witnessed the Sept. 19 Saskatoon, Saskatchewan show. "I was only fourteen at this show. My stepbrother had his driver's license, so we drove to Saskatoon from Melfort (where I grew up), about one hundred miles, on the afternoon of the show. It was the first 'big' rock concert for me. Previously, I had only seen the Stampeders at the Tisdale Arena, April Wine at the Melfort curling rink, and Chilliwack at our high school gym. It was also the first time I had ever seen people smoking pot. Nobody seemed to be going schizo, unlike what I had been told in health class.

"I had only heard the Rush songs 'In the Mood' and 'Fly By Night' on the radio but knew they had won a Juno for best new group just recently. *Caress Of Steel* was introduced as 'our new album coming out in a couple of weeks,' and it was the first Rush album I ever bought.

"During Neal Peart's solo, some idiot bounced a sparkler off his drum kit. They stopped the show, brought the house lights up, and threatened to cancel Nazareth if anything else hit the stage.

"I was a big Nazareth fan and had the *Razamanaz*, *Loud 'n' Proud*, *Rampant*, and *Hair of the Dog* albums. Didn't yet know about their first two albums. I thought I had them all at the time. I recall that they played every hit that I knew. The opening number was 'Changin' Times,' and the second was 'Razamanaz.' It was the first time I had ever seen a mirror ball (during 'Love Hurts') and explosions (during 'Shapes Of Things'). The old Saskatoon arena had a ceiling covered with raw asbestos. I was shaking it out of my hair and jacket after the show."

The band continued to support *Hair of the Dog* live on stage in 1976 with a thirty-three-date tour with Deep Purple in the US (who were promoting their *Come Taste The Band* album), which ran from January 14 in Largo to March 4 in Denver. At the January 23 stop at Radio City

Music Hall in New York, the band opened with "Changin' Times," which was given a powerful Led Zeppelin-style groove and the encore of "Teenage Nervous Breakdown," which led into a meaty cover of ZZ Top's "Tush."

Near the end of the tour, Deep Purple and Nazareth hit the Long Beach Arena in Long Beach, California, for a show that has been well documented, for one of the groups at least. Nazareth's set consisted of "Razamanaz," "This Flight Tonight," "Night Woman" (with a guitar intro from Charlton that comes close to quoting the Who's "Won't Get Fooled Again"), "Love Hurts," and "Woke Up This Morning."

After five more shows in March without Nazareth, Deep Purple disbanded.

RE-ISSUES, RE-MASTERS, AND RE-RECORDINGS

The Deep Purple portion of the February 27 show in Long Beach was released on CD in July 1995 as *King Biscuit Flower Hour Presents: Deep Purple in Concert* with four bonus tracks from Springfield on January 26 (at which Nazareth also performed). In February 2009, the February 27, 1976 show was re-released on CD as *Live At Long Beach Arena 1976*. No official live Nazareth release exist from this tour.

In 1997, Castle released *Hair of the Dog* on CD with four bonus tracks, the non-album tracks "Love Hurts," with its flip side "Down," the B-side to "Holy Roller," "Railroad Boy" (but strangely not the A-side), and the single edit of the album's title track, which cuts out the drum intro and fades out a bit early. The Castle version of the album also mislabels "Rose In The Heather" as "Rose In Heather."

The 2002 CD from Eagle Records presents those same four extra songs plus the non-album track "Holy Roller," a marginally alternate mix of the same song, and a single edit of "My White Bicycle," which is surely a fake (Why would a "single edit" even exist if the song has no album version?)

In 2010, Salvo issued their own version of *Hair of the Dog* with nine bonus tracks, including "Love Hurts," "My White Bicycle," "Holy Roller," and "Railroad Boy" plus an additional five songs recorded live at the Paris Theatre in London on November 27, 1975. The live portion has the band toughening their sound on "Hair of the Dog" (with Dan changing or forgetting some lyrics), "Holy Roller" (jokingly introduced as "Bay City Holy Rollers"), "Teenage Nervous Breakdown," "This Flight Tonight," and a rare cover of Frank Zappa's "Road Ladies," a bluesy lament about touring from his 1970 album *Chunga's Revenge*.

All of these compilations seem put together sloppily with not much thought going into the track listings. A much simpler set that would have made more sense is a two-CD set with one disc being the album plus the five, related, non-album tracks ("Love Hurts," "Down," "My White Bicycle," "Holy Roller," and "Railroad Boy"). The second disc would be the complete, ten-song November 27, 1975 live show, the first half which is on the 2011 boxed set *The Naz Box* and the last half on the Salvo reissue of *Hair of the Dog*. Additionally, three more songs from this show have not been released officially but could be added to present the complete concert. Fake alternate mixes and edits need not be included.

The legacy of *Hair of the Dog* lives on with not one but five notable cover versions of the title track in existence. In 1989, Philadelphia hair metal band Britny Fox included a predictably glammy rendition on their *Boys In Heat* album, while none other than Guns N' Roses did a grittier job on their all-covers album *The Spaghetti Incident?* in 1993. Warrant included their version of the song on their 2001 all-covers album *Under The Influence* (which also has a version of the Michael Monroe song "Dead, Jail or Rock 'n' Roll," which was originally on Monroe's *Not Fakin' It* release, the home of his cover of that Nazareth tune). The Warrant track sounds more like a cover of the Guns N' Roses version—a photocopy of a photocopy!

In 2005, the Michael Schenker Group featured the song on the all-covers album *Heavy Hitters* with ex-Iron Maiden belter Paul Di'anno handling lead vocals. This album was re-released in 2007 with the new title *Doctor Doctor: The Kulick Sessions* and again in 2011, this time called

By Invitation Only. The track listings for these reissues are both slightly different than that of *Heavy Hitters*, but all editions include "Hair of the Dog." Finally, in 2007, the group Kid Ego released their own sped-up version of the song, this rendition featuring backing vocals from Nazareth themselves.

While all of these versions are serviceable, none of them improve upon the original. Similarly, on her 1990 all-covers album, *The Hit List*, Joan Jett included a vocally restrained version of "Love Hurts." Considering other artists represented on the disc include AC/DC, Jimi Hendrix, the Doors, and ZZ Top, we'll assume she is covering the Nazareth arrangement and not the Everly Brothers. Jett's "Love Hurts" was released as a single with a music video to accompany it. It reached number one hundred on the UK charts.

The song "Please Don't Judas Me" was revived by Metallica in October 2007 when they performed a dramatic acoustic version at Neil Young's long-running Bridge School Benefit concert in Mountainview, California (where they also essayed "I Just Want To Celebrate" by Rare Earth and Blue Oyster Cult's "Veteran Of The Psychic Wars"). Metallica played it again on December. 5, 2011, in San Francisco as part of the band's thirtieth anniversary celebration concerts.

Dan McCafferty
1975

BACKGROUND

Before starting on their next album, Nazareth took a break to regroup. During this respite, Dan McCafferty began work on a solo project—not that he was taking the journey too far from home, as his partner in his day job, Manny Charlton, assumed production and lead guitar duties. Former Nazareth producer Roger Glover (*Razamanaz, Loud 'n' Proud,* and *Rampant*) provided bass guitar, and the Sensational Alex Harvey

(SAHB) band members Zal Cleminson, Hugh McKenna, and Ted McKenna played guitar, keyboards, and drums, respectively. Scottish pub rockers SAHB shared management with Nazareth, making the sessions for the McCafferty album a family affair. The musicians gathered at Basing Street Studios in London to record the album with later mixing taking place at Air Studios, also in London.

The format of the record showcased Dan's vocal range over a selection of carefully chosen cover songs. The assignment worked. *Dan McCafferty* (TOPS 102) was released in November 1975 and offered a wide sampling of the man's vocal talents. The cover illustration portrays a pensive looking McCafferty casually pouring wine into a goblet. The North American release sported a handsome photographic portrait of the artist.

ALBUM OVERVIEW

"The Honky Tonk Downstairs" starts with Glover's prominent bass guitar, giving away to a rollicking romp with suitably honky-tonk piano and then a varied twin guitar solo from Charlton and Cleminson. Written originally by Dallas Frazier, it appeared on George Jones' 1968 album *Sings The Songs Of Dallas Frazier*, although McCafferty and Charlton most likely learned it from the self-titled 1970 album by American country-rock band Poco.

Neil Young's "Cinnamon Girl" from his 1969 album *Everybody Knows This is Nowhere* album gets a light treatment with mournful organ playing and McCafferty almost whispering the familiar lyrics. Cleminson lets loose with two expressive solos near the end of the track.

On "The Great Pretender" (recorded originally by the Platters in 1955, the juxtaposition of hearing Dan's familiar raspy vocals over standard 1950s backing voices is a new context for the singer.

The second Bob Dylan cover of his career, "Boots Of Spanish Leather" (from 1964's *The Times They Are A-Changin'*), is a faithful rendition with warm Garth Hudson-style organ washes, unlike the drastic re-imagining that Nazareth brought to "The Ballad Of Hollis Brown" on *Loud 'n' Proud*. Still, McCafferty isn't too referential, leaning hard into portions of the lyrics with authority.

"Watcha Gonna Do About It" is a slight reggae tune with call and response solos between guitar and synthesizer. Originally recorded (and co-written) by Doris Troy, who had a number thirty-seven UK hit with it in 1964, the song also appeared on the Hollies' *Stay With The Hollies* album from the same year.

Next up is "Out Of Time" from the Rolling Stones' 1966 album *Aftermath*. (Chris Farlow had a number one UK hit with "Out Of Time" in 1966 as well.) It begins innocently enough with Dan taking his time enunciating the words until the chorus surges forward with competing horn players, a full string section, and soulful female backing vocals. McCafferty gives a near-Nazareth performance when spitting lyrics like "You're on your way out!"

A sawing fiddle gives "You Can't Lie To A Liar" a unique flavour on an album filled with them. A thumping beat accents Dan's vocal, which gets harsher as the song continues. The added value of the different instrumentation is a bonus. Ketty Wells first recorded "You Can't Lie To A Liar" in 1962.

Next is a vocal and piano-only ballad version of the song "Trouble" by Little Feat from their 1972 album *Sailin' Shoes*. The naked emotion of Dan's performance mirrors the lyrical concerns. Obviously, Little Feat's primary songwriter Lowell George was an important influence on McCafferty, this being the second cover he had done after "Teenage Nervous Breakdown" on Nazareth's 1973 *Loud 'n' Proud*.

The cover of Sam And Dave's 1966 tune "You Got Me Hummin'" comes across much heavier than the original by replacing heaving horns with a slithering guitar that flexes its muscle beneath the chorus.

This track could have fit comfortably on Nazareth records like *Loud 'n' Proud* or *Hair of the Dog*. McCafferty sings both Sam Moore and Dave Prater's parts.

The album ends triumphantly with a career high point for McCafferty in the form of the majestic ballad "Stay With Me Baby." McCafferty displays a welcomed sensitivity during the verses but, uplifted by a massive orchestra swelling and crashing, howls, "Stay with me baby!" in anguish during the dramatic choruses. His urgent declaration makes for an accomplished performance. "Stay With Me Baby" was recorded originally in 1966 by Lorraine Ellison, who filled in at a session when Frank Sinatra failed to show up.

RELEASE AND RECEPTION

Previewing the album was the single "Out Of Time" with "Cinnamon Girl" on the B-side (TOP 1), released in September 1975 and reaching number forty-one on the UK charts. The follow-up single, "Whatcha Gonna Do About It" (TOP 5), with the non-album single "Nightingale" on the B-side, only managed to secure the number fifty-one spot on the British chart. The three-track release "Stay With Me Baby," "Out Of Time," and "Whatcha Gonna Do About It" (DAN 1) and "Honky Tonk Downstairs" and "Trouble" (TOP 18) were also both released but without making any impressions on the charts.

In Scandinavia, "The Great Pretender" with "Stay With Me Baby" on the B-side was issued on Vertigo Records (6078 235). "Whatcha Gonna Do About It" was reissued in the UK (TOP 47), this time with "Boots Of Spanish Leather." This pairing was issued in Holland with a colourful cartoon sleeve (6079 037) and in Germany (6079 039) with a live shot of Dan on the sleeve. A promotional twelve-inch for "Whatcha Gonna Do About It" (also with "Boots Of Spanish Leather" on the flip side) was issued by Mountain Records (TOP 47 DJ) and featured a new mix that accented the track's reggae vibe with the addition of Jamaican musicians (guitar and horns), including famed rhythm team Sly Dunbar and Robbie Shakespeare plus ex-Wailers backing vocalists the I Threes (Rita Marley, Judy Mowatt, and Marcia Griffiths). Produced by Winston "Niney" Holness, this extended mix runs a full three and a half minutes longer than the original album recording. The remix has an effortless push-pull sensibility, although the extended portion past the four-minute mark is a far less noteworthy exercise in echo-laden dub.

In the US, a promotional single for "Out Of Time" was released featuring mono and stereo mixes on each side.

To promote the album, Dan made an appearance on the British TV show *Top Of The Pops,* performing a spirited version of "Out Of Time" (introduced incorrectly by notorious host Jimmy Savile as "Out Of Sight"). His old bandmates were also willing to help with promoting the album. A Nazareth concert at the Paris Theatre in London on November 27, 1975 featured the group (with Tommy Eyre on electric piano) offering heavy renditions of three songs from Dan's solo record.

On "Honky Tonk Downstairs," Dan sings with extra confidence from playing with his longtime bandmates. "Whatcha Gonna Do About It" has the rhythm section settling into the laid-back reggae groove while Dan's vocals are drenched in extra reverb. Finally, "You Got Me Hummin'" gets a tough Nazareth-styled fine tuning, bringing out an even heavier, lurching take than on the studio album. McCafferty adds an extra layer of snarl to his vocals while Charlton rips a particularly noisy guitar solo. Top-notch recordings of these three live songs appear on the four-CD boxed set *The Naz Box* (2011).

RE-ISSUES, RE-MASTERS, AND RE-RECORDINGS

In 2002, Eagle Records in Germany released *Dan McCafferty* along with his 1986 follow-up solo album *Into the Ring* as a two-CD set.

The debut album included an impressive seven additional tracks. Of them, the first is of primary interest. "Nightingale" was not only the B-side to the "Watcha Gonna Do About It" single, it's also notable for being an actual Nazareth outtake from the then-forthcoming album

Close Enough For Rock 'n' Roll. The track has a laid-back shuffling beat with slide guitar, and while the tune has a certain understated value, it's also easy to see why it didn't fit within the *Close Enough for Rock 'n' Roll* framework.

Other extra tracks on the Eagle Records CD are a single edit of "Watcha Gonna Do About It," which omits the piano intro and fades early to cut twenty seconds from the running time, and an alternate single edit of "Out Of Time" that just repeats all three verses and one chorus.

The liner notes claim that the bonus track of "Cinnamon Girl" is an unreleased extended version. In reality, it's yet another fake bonus song, where the second verse, chorus, and guitar solos all reappear at the point where the album version fades out.

Similarly, the alternate version of "Stay With Me Baby" just repeats the chorus one extra time near the end, while the alternate version of "The Honky Tonk Downstairs" simply trims the song's brief piano intro.

Also included is a "previously unreleased version" of "Watcha Gonna Do About It" that simply repeats the chorus and second verse, adding just over a minute to the. The previously mentioned "reggae version" extended mix of "Watcha Gonna Do About It" would have been a much preferred bonus track, but, unfortunately, it remains unavailable on CD. Having the three November 27, 1975 live songs would have overlapped with the *Naz Box* set but still would have made enough sense to justify their inclusion over the fake edits.

Salvo declined to make *Dan McCafferty* part of their Nazareth CD reissue series but then, in September 2013, released the album through iTunes. This digital download includes the B-side "Nightingale" but, thankfully, omits the six fake bonus tracks.

Finally, when a batch of Nazareth albums surfaced on counterfeit Russian two-for-one CDs in 1998, *Dan McCafferty* was paired with *Sound Elixir*.

Close Enough For Rock 'n' Roll

1976

BACKGROUND

Coming off the successful *Hair of the Dog* album and tour, including a thirty-three-date US tour from January to March opening for Deep Purple, who were promoting their *Come Taste the Band* album, the lads were ushered back into the studio to craft their seventh platter. With Manny Charlton running the boards once again, this time they hit Le Studio in Morin-Heights, Quebec, just northwest of Montreal.

Released in March 1976, *Close Enough For Rock 'n' Roll* (the band's first album on the Mountain label and issued as TOPS 109) stood out immediately when compared to their previous LPs. Where past records like *Razamanaz*, *Loud 'n' Proud* and *Hair of the Dog* were adorned with dynamic and colourful sleeves, the new LP arrived in an odd, grainy, black and white wraparound photo depicting the inside of a limousine surrounded by manic fans pressed against the windows. The reverse of the original gatefold sleeve revealed the band members huddled claustrophobically inside the encircled car. It's an eye-catching design, all the more so because of how different it is from the earlier covers.

ALBUM OVERVIEW

The record begins with a, new for Nazareth, crunching, four-part epic called "Telegram." Detailing life on the road for a hardworking rock combo, "Telegram" is an ambitious song composed of interconnecting mini-suites.

The first part of the story is the thumping "On Your Way." Aided by forceful piano playing from Pete Agnew, the band travels to a gig while listening to their own recording of "This Flight Tonight" on the limousine's FM radio, arriving at the hotel, and so on. The second installment, "So You Want To Be A Rock 'n' Roll Star," is simply a cover of the first verse of the song of that name by the Byrds from their 1967 album *Younger Than Yesterday*. The third part, "Sound Check," features a blistering guitar solo from Charlton and the lyric "Check guitars before you go, close enough for rock 'n' roll," giving the album it's title. The final part, "Here We Are Again," represents the band reaching the stage with appropriate crowd noise added.

What's strange is that after the typical Nazareth hard rock opening of "On Your Way," by the time they actually hit the stage, they sound more like Ringo Starr. Although multiple voices sing the pleasantly upbeat melody, one person is definitely singing the lead part, and it sure doesn't sound like McCafferty or Agnew. Could "Here We Are Again" be Darrell Sweet's debut as lead vocalist? It is a bit anti-climactic after the heavier previous chapters in the song. Tellingly, for years, this fourth part of the song was not played in concert when "Telegram" was slotted as the opening number.

"Vicki" is a brief acoustic guitar instrumental with folk-ish overtones. This gentle lullaby leads directly into the power chord-driven "Homesick Again." Bemoaning life on the road, "Homesick Again" pairs ringing lead guitar with an acoustic playing the rhythm part beneath while Pete shadows Dan's vocals during the verses.

"Vancouver Shakedown" is less a tribute to one of the many Canadian cities that supported the band early on than a dressing down of a west coast concert promoter who shortchanged the band twice. This arena-ready rant, with a rattling tambourine, is a virtual re-write of "Shanghai'd in Shanghai" from 1974's *Rampant*. The tune gets an extra surge of energy when McCafferty shouts. "But we got laid over!" at the bridge to each chorus while Sweet bashes away.

Next is "Born Under The Wrong Sign," a dark, shuffling tune that grinds along menacingly, although with some pretty funky bass playing from Agnew.

"Loretta" is a raunchy, little number with typically hoarse vocals from McCafferty and insistent guitar riffing followed by an airborne solo before returning to its previous tempo.

The album's poppier contribution to the catalogue follows. "Carry Out Feelings" has a great melody, slightly Caribbean percussion, mostly acoustic guitars, and gorgeous harmonies courtesy of McCafferty and Agnew. This has to be one of the group's most accessible original compositions with a chorus that practically demands you sing along.

"Lift The Lid," with it's driving boogie rhythm, is an early ZZ Top-influenced track with Bill Gibbons-style guitar riffing throughout. McCafferty's inimitable vocals are the only thing grounding the track in Nazareth territory. Along with the many American groups that influenced Nazareth, this song shows a clear debt to the Texas trio.

The album ends satisfyingly with a Jeff Barry cover, "You're the Violin," featuring a heavy but still melodic guitar solo from Charlton. "You're the Violin" had been recorded previously in 1974 by ex-professional football player turned actor Rosie Grier.

RELEASE AND RECEPTION

Close Enough for Rock 'n' Roll peaked at number twelve in Canada, achieving gold certification, and at number twenty-four on the US charts (SP-4562). "Carry Out Feelings," with "Lift The Lid" on the B-side, was released as a single in the UK (TOP 8) and North America (1819 on A&M Records) in February 1976, barely managing to hit number seventy-nine in Canada.

A theory as to how an almost perfectly constructed pop song could fail in North America may be that the lyrical comparison of a doomed relationship to fast food lost something in translation. The terms "carry out" and "take away" are not common in America, where the more familiar phrase "take out" is used to describe cheap food on the go. A radio promo single for "Carry Out Feelings" featured the stereo mix on the A-side and a mono version on the B-side. The "Carry Out Feelings" single was also released in Holland and Portugal with "Lift The Lid" on the B-side and with "Railroad Boy" on the flip-side in Australia.

The guys filmed a basic music video for the song, miming along to the track on stage while bathed in pale blue light. The stereo/mono Canadian single for "Loretta" (1854 on A&M) only managed to reach number eight-four, while "You're the Violin" was released as a single (TOP 14) with "Loretta" on the B-side in the UK but with no chart action at all. The mono mixes of "Carry Out Feelings" and "Loretta" have never been released on CD. Malaysia issued a seven-inch single of

"You're the Violin" (JBRE 149) to be played on jukeboxes. This release features Albert Hammond on the B-side with his single "Moonlight Lady" from the 1976 album *When I Need You*.

Back on the road, the significant lineup of Nazareth, Thin Lizzy, and Ian Gillan stormed the Aragon Ballroom in Chicago on June 4, 1976 for a night of hard rock dominance. On June 10 in Omaha, Slade was added to that trio of hard rock heroes.

On June 11, 1976, the band played a barnstorming headlining set at the St. Paul Civic Center in St. Paul Minneapolis. The show kicks off with "Telegram." Although known now as a frequent opening number, at that point it was still a new song for the audience. During "Bad Bad Boy," Dan mentions "a St. Paul girl" in the lyrics while "Loved And Lost" features a gripping, extended guitar solo. Speaking of Charlton, "Changin' Times" has a long guitar jam at the end that the band should have explored more often. "Hair of the Dog" begins with some slightly different guitar parts, sounding not unlike the Beatles' "Day Tripper" for a few bars.

Incredibly, as strong as *Close Enough* is, forty years after its original release, "Telegram" is the only song from it Nazareth has performed in concert. Surely "Vancouver Shakedown" would have gotten a positive response even if for the wrong reasons if tested in front of a Canadian crowd.

Tragedy struck on July 28 1976 when manager Bill Fehilly was killed (along with five others, including Fehilly's young son and the pilot) while traveling by small plane from Blackpool, Lancashire to Scotland. The plane went down just after crossing the Scottish border. This setback affected the band personally and professionally, since Fehilly had been such an early supporter. It took years to sort through all of the various business holdings he controlled.

RE-ISSUES, RE-MASTERS, AND RE-RECORDINGS

The 1998 Castle CD has three bonus tracks, including the 1971 non-album single "Holy Roller" (which has absolutely nothing to do with *Close Enough for Rock 'n' Roll*), a DJ edit of "You're the Violin," and the so-called US single edit of "Carry Out Feelings." Of these, "You're the Violin" fades out early and surely was not actually considered for release as a single, making it a fake bonus song, and the "US single edit" of "Carry Out Feelings" is no different from the album cut, making it an inauthentic additional track as well.

In 2002, Eagle Records released their own CD edition (using the same liner notes from the Castle disc), which was bolstered with a supposedly generous seven extra songs. There are two single versions of the non-album track "My White Bicycle," the DJ edit of "You're the Violin," and the US edit of "Carry Out Feelings." There are also single edits of "Loretta," "Lift The Lid," and "Telegram." In a blasphemous move, this cut of "Loretta" removes the guitar solo, "Lift The Lid" has an early fade, and "Telegram" fades after the "So You Want To Be A Rock 'n' Roll Star" segment. These are all fake bonus tracks created purely to add content to the CD reissues except for the odd "Telegram" edit, which appeared on the B-side to the 1979 single "Whatever You Want, Babe" in Portugal.

Salvo combined their 2010 release of *Close Enough . . .* with the follow-up record *Play 'n' the Game* on one disc, having to omit any bonus tracks for the former due to space restrictions. Considering how Castle and Eagle Records approached supplemental material for this title, perhaps that was a good thing.

Play 'n' the Game
1976

BACKGROUND

During a cross-country Canadian tour, the band were presented with multiple awards at a September 24, 1976 stop in Edmonton, Alberta, including gold albums for *Rampant* and *Close Enough for Rock 'n' Roll*, platinum albums for *Razamanaz* and *Loud 'n' Proud*, double platinum for *Greatest Hits*, and even a gold single for "Love Hurts." The treadmill Nazareth had been on for years—album, tour, album tour—continued, but the gears were finally grinding down.

After six months of touring to promote *Close Enough for Rock 'n' Roll*, the band went directly into Le Studio again, but this time without any songs. With Charlton still handling production duties, Nazareth scrambled to come up with enough material for their next full-length platter. When released in November 1976, *Play 'n' the Game* (TOPS 113) showed how much of a struggle it had been.

ALBUM OVERVIEW

The album opens optimistically with "Somebody to Roll," a chugging, mid-tempo rocker with especially ragged lead vocals and a multi-track guitar solo from Charlton.

Alvin Robinson's 1964 hit "Down Home Girl" gets a suitably raunchy arrangement, surely learned from the 1965 Rolling Stones cover. It appeared on their UK album *The Rolling Stones No. 2* and the US equivalent *The Rolling Stones Now!*, also from 1965. The guitar solo is a better than average effort from Charlton.

"Flying" has similar subject matter to "This Flight Tonight" and is notable for McCafferty's gliding vocals. This slight alteration it really too much of a retread of the earlier hit without the intended results. (It wasn't even released as a single.)

"Waiting For The Man" opens with an extremely funky bass guitar over a swinging rhythm, while an engaging McCafferty vocal details the colourful exploits of a street corner gang. The macho posturing doesn't really fit the band's image at that point, but I can't argue with that bass.

"Born To Love" is a low and dirty rumbler with the band moving things forward briskly. Charlton provides a tasteful blur of notes for his brief solo.

The highlight of the album is the cover of Joe Tex's "I Want To Do Everything For You," a steady, bluesy number that became a regular part of the band's live set for years. In 1965, Tex hit number one on the R&B chart and number twenty-three on the pop chart with this song.

"I Don't Want To Go On Without You" is a tentative ballad with California-style harmonies that could have fit comfortably on Dan's solo album from the previous year, although that record already has enough of that sort of high school dance material.

A seemingly odd source of inspiration, "Wild Honey," takes The Beach Boys' typically sunny disposition and gives it a uniquely dark treatment, employing odd instrumentation and a truly bloodcurdling scream from McCafferty.

The album finishes with "LA Girls," a quick, little rocker with handclaps, prominent bass guitar, and a flurry of notes for the guitar solo. The number ends with the waning sound of a distorted guitar , followed by the sudden, sharp pop of a shattered light bulb. The band also attempted a cover of "Wild Tiger Woman" by the Move, but that recording has not surfaced anywhere.

The record sleeve abandons the dramatic illustrations of *Loud 'n' Proud* and *Hair of the Dog* for a shot of the four lads glaring at the viewer for daring to interrupt what looks like a serious game of cards.

Of the nine songs on the album, the band has only played "Born To Love" and "I Want To Do Everything For You" live, although in the case of the latter, it has been played *a lot*.

RELEASE AND RECEPTION

Upon release in November 1976 (and dedicated to recently deceased manager Bill Fehilly), *Play 'n' the Game* reached number seventy-five on the US charts and number fourteen in Canada, going gold.

"I Don't Want To Go On Without You" was released as a single in the UK, Norway, Portugal, Holland, Spain, and Japan with the unreleased track "Good Love" on the B-side.

It's hard to believe that for an album lacking consistently strong material, an extra tune, "Good Love," was not used. The song has a rough, early AC/DC guitar riff and is certainly no weaker than some of the stuff that made it onto the record. Why it was regulated to the B-side of a single when it could have replaced any one of at least four album cuts and made *Play 'n' The Game* stronger is anyone's guess.

"I Don't Want To Go On Without You" was also released as a single in Germany and South Africa but with "LA Girls" on the B-side. A promotional twelve-inch for the song had "Waiting For The Man" on the flip. In Barbados "Born To Love" appeared as a single paired with "I Don't Want To Go On Without You" as the B-side. "Somebody To Roll," with "Vancouver Shakedown" from 1976's *Close Enough For Rock 'n' Roll*. was released as a single in the UK, while in Brazil, "Flying" backed with "Loretta" (also from *Close Enough*...) appeared on seven-inch vinyl.

A summer 1977 North American tour included a massive show at Anaheim Stadium in California on June 19 with the Tubes, Sha Na Na, Nazareth, and the Kinks supporting headliner Alice Cooper, who was promoting his *Lace And Whiskey* album. An edited version of the concert was broadcast on television in September under the title *Alice Cooper and Friends,* showing Nazareth performing "This Flight Tonight," "Love Hurts." and "Loved And Lost" from the *Rampant* album. Heavily intoxicated, Cooper is not served as well by the footage. Although available briefly on VHS, *Alice Cooper and Friends* has never been reissued on any home video format.

Further summer dates had Nazareth opening for Aerosmith on their *Draw the Line* tour.

RE-ISSUES, RE-MASTERS, AND RE-RECORDINGS

Nazareth was featured on a promotional-only sampler album put out by their old label Mountain Records. *Mountain Rocks Into '77* (PSLP 200) showcased two songs by Nazareth ("Somebody To Roll" and "I Want To Do Everything For You"), SAHB Without Alex ("Big Boy," "Pick It Up And Kick It") Ginger Baker and Friends, and Krazy Kat.

The 1999 release of *Play 'n' The Game* on CD from Castle Music features four bonus tracks: the non-album B-side "Good Love," an alternate edit of "I Don't Want To Go On Without You," a promo-only twelve-inch alternate edit of "Waiting For The Man," and an edited version of "Somebody To Roll." The promo "I Don't Want To Go On Without You" repeats the first half of the song at the end where the album version fades.

In 2002, Eagle Records released their version with the same alternative edits of "I Don't Want To Go On Without You" and "Waiting For The Man" and the edited "Somebody To Roll." This release also includes a fake edit of "Born To Love."

The 2010 CD release from Salvo pairs *Play 'n' The Game* with *Close Enough For Rock 'n' Roll* on one disc, leaving room only for the non-album B-side "Good Love."

and Agnew engage in call-and-response vocals during the chorus, barking "Expect no mercy!" at each other. The middle section has the band stopping and starting with road-tested agility and then jumping right back into the action-packed chorus.

The album's first cover, "Gone Dead Train," done originally by Crazy Horse on their self-titled 1971 debut album, is played at a similar pace as the template but with effective handclaps and solid backing vocals.

Written by Manny Charlton, "Shot Me Down" is a mid-tempo number with jangly guitars, a rattling tambourine, and Agnew's bass guitar high in the mix.

A flat-out rocker, "Revenge Is Sweet" (another Charlton composition) is most notable for a truly evil-sounding lead vocal from McCafferty. The guitar riff mirrors the staccato elements of the vocal track.

One of the five new songs done for the album, "Gimme What's Mine," is a perky, little number with an unrelenting, interlocking guitar and bass foundation over which Charlton solos.

The heavy blues with booming drums of "Kentucky Fried Blues" slithers along with a classic Charlton guitar figure. Somehow, McCafferty adds an extra abrasive layer to his lead vocals on this track.

"New York Broken Toy" is similar in structure to "Gimme What's Mine" but with more impassioned soloing from Charlton. McCafferty is in fine voice, suitably gravelly but not at the expense of being expressive.

The cover of "Busted" (done famously by Johnny Cash in 1963 on his *Blood, Sweat And Tears* album and also a hit for Ray Charles the same year on the *Ingredients In A Recipe For Soul* release) is a sort of humorous electric blues, and there's absolutely nothing wrong with that, but these guys can do this sort of thing in their sleep.

The next track, "Place In Your Heart," is also new to the project. The song is an odd addition to the supposedly heavier version of the album, as it's a poppy track with acoustic guitars (not unlike "Carry Out Feelings" from *Close Enough For Rock 'n' Roll*), and Dan displays some of his cleanest vocals on record. "Place In Your Heart" is also the third and final song on the album credited solely to Charlton.

Another new song, "All The King's Horses," is a regal epic with a foundation of acoustic rhythm guitars over which Charlton wails. Thematically, this is sort of a sequel to "The King Is Dead' from *Nazareth* (1971), but we would have to hear them played back to back live to cement the connection.

RELEASE AND RECEPTION

With the album out, the band went into high gear to promote it. The first single, "Gone Dead Train" (NAZ 2), with tracks from the previous, unreleased incarnation of the album, "Greens" and "Desolation Road," hit number forty-nine on the UK charts, while the follow-up "Place In Your Heart" with "Kentucky Fried Blues" as the B-side (TOP 37) managed to reach only number seventy at home but an impressive number three in South Africa, although it was released as a single in Germany and Holland as well. A US single for "Gone Dead Train" was backed with "Kentucky Fried Blues," which was also the B-side to an American single for the song "Shot Me Down." Additionally, a US promotional single on A&M Records (2009) had mono and stereo mixes of "Shot Me Down." A twelve-inch US promo sampler (SP-4666-SPECIAL) for the album consisted of the tracks "Expect No Mercy," "Gone Dead Train," "Kentucky Fried Blues," "Busted," and "Shot Me Down."

Relatively new at the time, rudimentary music videos were shot for "Place In Your Heart" and "Shot Me Down," which featured the guys miming to the songs in the recording studio and onstage. Rush fans will recognize the setting from that band's 1981 "Tom Sawyer" music video, also shot at Le Studio.

As usual, Nazareth hit the road to bring the music to the people, although only four songs from the album were aired in a live setting, including the title track, "Gone Dead Train," "Kentucky Fried Blues," and "New York Broken Toy."

On November 24, Nazareth played Golders Green Hippodrome in London. During the gig, Dan introduces "Gone Dead Train," saying,

"We have a new album out this week." Also included are a down and dirty "Kentucky Fried Blues" and an energetic sprint though the new title track. They also played a strong "Born To Love" from *Play 'n' The Game* and ended with "Whisky Drinkin' Woman," slamming immediately into a furious version of "Hair of the Dog."

The extensive North American headlining tour had several notable appearances. On February 7, 1978, Nazareth played the famed Cobo Hall in Detroit with Sammy Hager as the opening act. The band's nineteen-song set included four from the latest album. An excellent rendition of "New York Broken Toy" used echo on the vocals to great effect. "Kentucky Fried Blues," "Gone Dead Train," and a killer run-through the title track have smoking electric guitar work and prominent backing vocals. Other highlights of the Detroit gig are the long, bluesy intro to "I Want To Do Everything For You" and extensive slide guitar on "Cocaine." The recording of this show documents Dan and the guys commanding the arena with authority. If released officially, this 1978 Detroit concert would be a definitive record of the original band at their performing peak.

As the tour reached California in March 1978, McCafferty performed some shows (confirmed as occurring in Fresno and Santa Monica) in a stationary, seated position, apparently due to a back injury sustained in a recent car accident.

In the spring, the band embarked on an ambitious cross-Canada tour, hitting large and small markets, endearing themselves further to that particularly loyal fan base. The opening act on this tour alternated between the UK act Be-Bop Deluxe and the legendary Canadian band the Guess Who, promoting their then-new album *Guess Who's Back*, the group's first without front man Burton Cummings.

On May 1, Jim Hansen saw the tour at the Montreal Forum with Be-Bop Deluxe in the opening slot. Here are his recollections: "I was front row, to the side, and totally engulfed by the dry ice as they opened with 'Telegram.' Believe it or not, the entire Forum was packed. I'll never forget the flash pots during 'Shapes Of Things.' I bought a large Nazareth *Expect No Mercy* button, which I still have!"

The Toronto show on May 3 was witnessed by Murray Herstig: "Seeing Nazareth in concert at Maple Leaf Gardens back in 1978 was one of the highlights of my life. I remember a galaxy of stars spinning around the Gardens as a laser beam of white light was reflected off a giant mirror ball hanging above the center of the stage. While the band was playing 'This Flight Tonight,' I felt this otherworldly experience come over me. To this day, I still enjoy listening to Nazareth music, and I love *Expect No Mercy*."

RE-ISSUES, RE-MASTERS, AND RE-RECORDINGS

Portions of the dynamic Golders Green Hippodrome concert (originally recorded and filmed as part of the BBC Sight & Sound series) have been released in pieces over the years. The 1998 two-CD collection *At The Beeb* has five of the tracks, while six other songs from the show were released on the 2011 four-CD set *The Naz Box*. The 2005 DVD *In The Beginning* has historically valuable footage of twelve songs performed, although, unfortunately, "Gone Dead Train" is omitted while "Razamanaz" and "I Want To Do Everything For You" have been added. *From The Beginning* also has the music videos for "Shot Me Down" and "Place In Your Heart."

A unique double album compilation entitled *Place In Your Heart* (DAR 215) was released in South Africa in 1978. This set had all the expected favourites plus a few odd choices, such as "Fool About You," "Born Under The Wrong Sign," and "All The King's Horses."

The 1998 Castle *Expect No Mercy* CD has two great bonus tracks: the B-sides "Greens" and "Desolation Road."

In 2002, Eagle Records released their own CD, keeping the two Castle B-sides but adding edited versions of "Gone Dead Train" and "Kentucky Fried Blues" plus alternate versions of "Expect No Mercy" and "Place In Your Heart." While these edited and alternate takes are suspect, one worthwhile extra song on the Eagle Records CD is a previously unreleased live recording of "Expect No Mercy." This live version is especially bombastic, but, unfortunately, no information is provided regarding the source of this exceptional take.

In 2010, Salvo issued a deluxe edition CD that, incredibly, presented the previously unreleased, rejected version of the ten-song album. A true treasure trove for fans, this "second" album sheds new light on the behind-the-scenes decisions made regarding the band's career at that time.

This sheltered album begins with "Kentucky Fried Blues" but then has different versions of "Gone Dead Train" and "Shot Me Down." The second version of "Gone Dead Train" is a definite improvement over this earlier take, which has some tentative banjo-styled picking and solo on guitar. The original "Shot Me Down" also has a country-styled guitar solo and gentle backing vocals and is played at a slower tempo than the album version. Next is the heavy riffing of "Greens," which had been issued as a B-side to the single "Gone Dead Train." The guitar solo on this is Scottish-sounding, almost replicating the tone of traditional bagpipes. Fifth on the unreleased album is "Life Of A Dog," a song that was left off the finished release. The song has Dan's corroded pipes over a bed of echo-drenched acoustic guitars and hard electric guitar riffs. "New York Broken Toy" and "Revenge Is Sweet" appear next, as they exist on the finished release. Another B-side, "Desolation Road," is also from the aborted album. This steady, mid-tempo cut with additional percussion has no relation to Bob Dylan's 1965 song "Desolation Row," although these guys are such big Dylan fans it's unlikely that the title is a coincidence. Next is "Can't Keep A Good Man Down," an odd track unlike anything the band had attempted at that point in their career. The tune boasts piercing guitar shards, tribal drumming, gang vocals, and handclaps during the chorus, but a near impermeable fog envelopes the track, resisting human contact. The murk has a hypnotic effect on the listener, drawing one into this anomaly in the massive Nazareth catalogue. The rejected platter ends with "Moonlight Eyes," a big ballad with piano (by Agnew?) that was a fave of Manny Charlton, but it's easy to see how this didn't fit the requested hard rock design of the project.

Comparing the two versions of the album opens up a series of questions. First of all, the idea that this earlier version was rejected because it wasn't "heavy" enough is problematic. Granted, the re-recordings of "Gone Dead Train" and "Shot Me Down" are far superior to what was on the initial tapes, and it's okay that "Place In Your Heart" on the finished album is not a hard rock songt by any means (neither is "Shot Me Down"), but both add variety and character to the album without obscuring the mission at hand. But it's difficult to fathom that in a desire for a heavier record, someone thought that a monstrous slab like "Greens" or even "Can't Keep A Good Man Down" should be replaced with a clearly lesser tune like "Busted." If one wanted a truly hard and heavy version of *Expect No Mercy*, the track listing would be something like:

1 – Expect No Mercy
2 – Gone Dead Train
3 – Shot Me Down
4 – Revenge Is Sweet
5 – Gimme What's Mine
6 – Place In Your Heart
7 – New York Broken Toy
8 – Greens
9 – Desolation Road
10 – Can't Keep A Good Man Down

While we're on the topic, a respectable deluxe edition would be a two-CD set with the second disc being the complete November 24, 1977 London recording.

No Mean City
1979

BACKGROUND

A major change in the Nazareth narrative occurred after the successful *Expect No Mercy* headlining arena tour. For the first time in the band's eleven-year history, there was an addition (not a replacement, like many other groups were experiencing around this time) to the proven four-man lineup. Manny Charlton was interested in sharing guitar duties, because he was being kept busy between songwriting, production, and axe work. Flamboyant Scottish guitar hero Zal Cleminson was the near-perfect fit. As a former member of the Sensational Alex Harvey Band, who shared management with Nazareth, Cleminson was already familiar to the guys. Perhaps more importantly, Charlton knew what to expect in the studio from the new recruit, having shared guitar duties and produced him for the 1975 *Dan McCafferty* sessions. Although he wouldn't be wearing the gleaming jumpsuits and mime-like makeup that was his SAHB trademark, Cleminson would still be a strong visual focal point for audiences with his animated stage presence.

The newly-formed quintet settled close to home at Ballostowelle Farm on the Isle Of Man for the recording of the debut album by this lineup and Charlton's fifth production credit. Further sessions for finished vocals and final mixing took place at Mountain Recording Studio in Montreux, Switzerland.

No Mean City (TOPS 123) was released in January of 1979, sporting another eye-catching cover sleeve, typical of the time.

ALBUM OVERVIEW

The rejuvenated group make themselves known immediately with "Just To Get Into It," a frantic stormer with Dan's vocals pushed unusually far back in the mix. This was not progress, folks. Why producer Charlton disarmed his most potent weapon on the opening track is baffling; however, the track does have a particularly high-velocity solo from Cleminson.

Next up is "May The Sunshine," which opens with chiming mandolin, slashing electric chords, and a memorable chorus with gang vocals that actually precede the first verse. During the fadeout is some interesting Indian-sounding guitar, a new source of inspiration for Nazareth. The full-bodied "Simple Solution parts 1 & 2" (credited solely to Cleminson) has a terrific swinging riff and one of Dan's most sandpaper-like screams when he hits the last word in the line "Send me down a simple solution *now*!"

The last cut on side one of the original vinyl is "Star," a mid-tempo track with a slightly flanged acoustic guitar, electric bursts, prominent bass, and stacked vocal harmonies.

"Claim To Fame" thuds along with a Neanderthal groove, phlegmy vocals, and some air raid siren tones from the guitar squadron. Along the more radio-friendly lines of "May The Sunshine," "Whatever You Want Babe" pulsates with a bouncing melody and detailed guitar work from Charlton and Cleminson. The track's pop sensibilities are countered by McCafferty's whisky-soaked croak.

For "What's In It For Me," tribal drums support McCafferty, who scowls over Charlton's wailing slide guitar.

No Mean City is capped off with the sprawling (well, for Nazareth) epic title track. This example of hard rock pageantry crashes into existence with some vintage Stones-styled guitars and a straight ahead, four-four drumbeat while McCafferty relates his tale of subterranean desolation. Just beneath the surface are some odd, barely distinguishable guitar sound effects, adding unsettling shades to the murky canvas. The bridge has a sudden, majestic tone to it, and then it's back to the solid drums and an oddly-picked guitar. A brief interlude breakdown sounds slightly Hawaiian, and soon afterwards, the song ends with spare guitar notes cascading gently during the fadeout. The title is taken from the 1935 novel *No Mean City: A Story of the Glasgow Slums* by H. Kingsley Long and Alexander McArthur.

RELEASE AND RECEPTION

"May The Sunshine," with "Expect No Mercy" on the B-side, was released as a single (NAZ 003) in the UK and reached number twenty-two on the charts. It also appeared as a single in Italy, South Africa, the Netherlands, Holland, Germany and Japan. "Star" with "Born To Love" on the B-side (TOP 45) hit number fifty-four in the UK and was also a single in Sweden.

"Whatever You Want Babe," backed with "Telegram" (of all things), was released as a single in the UK (NAZ 004) and in Portugal (6079 034). The UK version used the first three parts of "Telegram" as the B-side, whereas the Portuguese release only has the first two parts to the four-chambered track. In the US, both "May The Sunshine" and "Whatever You Want Babe" had promotional singles released with mono and stereo mixes on each side (2116 and 2130 respectfully). A&M Records also released a promotional EP called *Top Tracks* (SP-17062) that consisted of "May The Sunshine," "Whatever You Want Babe," and "What's In It For Me."

No Mean City reached number thirty-four on the UK charts, number eighty-eight in the US, and number eighty-one in Canada, where it achieved gold certification. The tracks "Star," "Whatever You Want Babe" and "What's In It For Me" have never been performed live by the band. This means that, in the case of the first two tracks, for some reason the band was not promoting two of the singles released to help push the album, a curious marketing approach, if there ever was one.

The same month the album was released, Nazareth appeared on BBC TV's *Top Of The Pops*, where they performed "May The Sunshine." Sure, they were lip-syncing, but any footage of the Zal era lineup is to be cherished.

After a few select live UK shows, they left for another North American tour. With opening act Thin Lizzy, they played over twenty shows throughout the US while also making appearances at some large music festivals. (Members of both bands went to see a concert by the Police in Houston on March 8.) On June 2, they appeared at the Mississippi River Jam II in Davenport, IA with Heart, AC/DC, UFO, and TKO. June 9 was the Texxas Jam in Dallas with Boston, Heart, Van Halen, Sammy Hagar, and Blue Oyster Cult, and on July 2, they appeared at the Canadian World Music Festival in Toronto with Ted Nugent, Aerosmith, Johnny Winter, Goddo, Triumph, Moxy, April Wine, and the Ramones, who were, infamously, pelted with garbage from the mostly hard rock fan base in attendance.

Part of their February 17 gig at the Blow Up in Luxembourg was broadcast on local radio. After "I Want To Do Everything For You," Dan introduces their new member, saying, "A friend of ours for a long time . . . Zal Cleminson!" They follow that with two songs from the new album, a ripping "Just To Get Into It" and "May The Sunshine." A surprise in the set is "Wrong Time," the Spooky Tooth cover they used to play in the early days. Interestingly, "Love Hurts" gets a heavy guitar treatment, unlike versions played on other tours. After that, they actually tackle the challenging title track from the new release, "No Mean City," which is notable for the rare live airing but also for how terrific it sounds in concert. The group rises easily to the task of recreating this complex, multi-tiered piece live. "Hair of the Dog" has a false start, but once they get going, it is a very confident version. A major difference is that Dan's voice-box solo is replaced with a traditional guitar solo, a rare occurrence indeed.

The band's first tour of Japan was documented at the May 16 concert in Tokyo. They give "Just To Get Into It" an extra surge of energy and open "No Mean City" with some extended expressive guitar playing. A firm reading of "Cocaine" is followed by a long intro into an excellent version of "Wrong Time." Charlton and Cleminson engage in some extended crisscrossing soloing during "Born To Lose," and Dan's vocals during "Shapes Of Things" sound even sharper than usual. Interestingly, the group reprises the intro to "Cocaine" at the beginning of "Love Hurts." The show finishes with a decent run-through of ZZ Top's "Tush."

On July 4, the band was part of a multi-artist festival at Oakland Stadium in Oakland California. The All American Rock & Roll Show, as it was called, featured Journey, the J. Geils Band, and the obviously "non-all-American" acts UFO, Thin Lizzy, and, of course, Nazareth.

RE-ISSUES, RE-MASTERS, AND RE-RECORDINGS

The 1998 CD reissue from Castle has three bonus tracks: single edits of "May The Sunshine" and "Whatever You Want Babe" plus the US version of "Star." The 2002 Eagle Records version includes the US "Star" plus an alternate edit of "No Mean City" and an edited version of "Simple Solution." The "No Mean City" alternate edit is a fake hatchet job that removes three verses from the middle of this ambitious album track. The "Simple Solution" edit is slightly shorter, omitting the semi-spoken bridge ("and the price of life...") portion.

Salvo responded in 2010 with an edition that sported just two extra tracks. The single mix of "May The Sunshine" is about a minute shorter than the album version, cutting the unique intro chorus, but the final song "Snaefell" (named for the highest mountain on the Isle Of Man) is a gem. A joint collaboration between the freshly-forged guitar duo of Charlton and Cleminson, the instrumental tune should have made it onto the album. It would have added some poetic character and showcased the new team working together. Perhaps its obvious resemblance to "Definitely Maybe" from the Jeff Beck Group's self-titled album from 1972 kept it off the finished record. Regardless, swapping it with one of the slightly lesser songs ("Star" maybe?) and then moving it to either proceed or follow the title track would have added to the record's conceptual design.

The liner notes to the Salvo release incorrectly credit Frank Frazetta with the cover art. The dramatic illustration is actually the work of Rodney Matthews, who went on to design album sleeves for Magnum, Asia, and others.

Malice In Wonderland
1980

BACKGROUND

The addition of the dynamic Zal Cleminson gave Nazareth a shot in the arm, but instead of building on that momentum, they decided on another major switch-up. Guitarist Manny Charlton had produced the proceeding five albums but would not be helming the latest work. Instead, that responsibility went to Jeff "Skunk" Baxter of Steely Dan and the Doobie Brothers fame, effectively neutering the twin firepower of the Charlton-Cleminson alliance. The setting also changed drastically, with the band and producer heading down to Compass Point Studios in the Barbados to record—or maybe just to enjoy the sun.

After a few weeks at Compass Point, they traveled to Mountain Recording Studio in Montreux, Switzerland to finish the vocal tracks and final mixing chores. When released in February 1980 *Malice in Wonderland* (TOPS 126) displayed the results of all these changes.

ALBUM OVERVIEW

An immediate Nazareth fan favourite, "Holiday" opens the album with an upbeat melody and supremely catchy chorus. Amidst the "pop" concessions, Dan still shows a glint of his usual menace when he spits the line, "I don't know who my daddy is!"

"Showdown At The Border" could have worked if not rendered so toothless, and the breakdown portion in the middle is just awkward. Apparently, one of Baxter's directives was for choruses to just be the song title repeated endlessly. Next is "Talkin' To One Of The Boys," another track that goes nowhere with odd-sounding backing vocals that are saved somewhat by an interesting Zal Cleminson guitar solo.

"Heart's Grown Cold," credited solely to Cleminson, although Pete Agnew claims to have written the majority of the lyrics, is a mostly acoustic ballad with female backing vocals. It begins with delicate guitar picking from Cleminson, Charlton, and Baxter and a pleading lead vocal courtesy of McCafferty. The soulful backing vocals join in just as Sweet's drums swell for added dramatic effect. For the type of song it is and what it wants to convey, its construction is nearly flawless. From a pure songwriting point of view, it's easily the strongest cut on the album.

A mysterious film noir mood permeates "Fast Cars," but it's hard not to get thrown by the fact that vibes player Alan Estes is on the track, and that he actually takes the solo on the song while a bloody virtuoso like Cleminson is tethered nearby.

"Big Boy" begins with an acceptable riff (Charlton the producer surely would have toughened up Charlton the guitar player), which leads inexplicably to a reggae chorus and then back again. A braying tenor saxophone solo hammers home the producer's—not the band's—aesthetic. This song is one that Cleminson brought to the band, having recorded previously as a member of SAHB—without Alex on the 1977 album *Fourplay*. Musically, the original version trumps the Nazareth cover except for the lead vocals department, where Dan, naturally, comes out on top.

An above-average guitar solo is about all that stands out on the funky "Talkin' Bout Love," while "Fallen Angel" is a decent enough mid-tempo cut that has Dan sounding engaged with the material. A heavy-handed string section rises in the mix on this one. "Ship Of Dreams" is exactly the kind of low-key, LA-smooth rock to be expected from "Skunk" Baxter, but it is completely at odds with the established identity of the working-class Scots who make up the band. The album ends with "Turning A New Leaf," a tune with the potential for heaviness, to which Baxter seems oblivious. McCafferty turns in a soft lead vocal, mostly without any of his trademark rasp, but there's an odd gating effect on the drums that is distracting.

RELEASE AND RECEPTION

Once out, *Malice In Wonderland* reached number forty-one in the US, number forty-three in Germany, number nine in Norway, and number nineteen in Canada, where it went gold, all of which means *Malice* actually performed better on the charts than either *Expect No Mercy* or *No Mean City*! This encouragement would only lead to further frustration for fans. In Mexico, the album was released as *O Anos De Musica Rock—Salvat* (822 304 1) and had a full colour cover sleeve photo of the five-man band in concert.

The seven-inch single for "Holiday," with "Ship Of Dreams" on the flip side (TOP 50), reached number eight-seven in the US and number twenty-one in Canada (where it was awarded gold certification) and was also released in Holland and Spain. A different "Holiday" single, this one with "Talkin' Bout Love" (6079 042) on the flip side, was released in Germany, France, Guatemala, South Africa, and Mexico. In Holland, "Big Boy" paired with "Turning A New Leaf" was released as a single (6000 434). The album tracks "Fast Cars," "Talkin' Bout Love," "Fallen Angel," "Ship Of Dreams," and "Turning A New Leaf" have never been performed live by the band.

While promoting the new album on tour, one concert achieved near legendary status. Part of the band's March 16, 1980 show at the

Hammersmith Odeon in London, where they played exactly half of the new, ten-song album, was broadcast on the BBC's *Rock Hour* radio program, and portions were released throughout the years. The original radio broadcast consisted of full-throttle versions of "Razamanaz," "I Want To Do Everything For You," "Showdown At The Border," "Heart's Grown Cold," "Big Boy," "Holiday," "This Flight Tonight," "Hair of the Dog," "Talkin' To One Of The Boys," "Expect No Mercy," and "Broken Down Angel." This recording is the first professionally-captured tape of the five-man group in action, and listeners were not disappointed by the quality of their performance.

The broadcast begins with a BBC DJ stating that the group is "one of Scotland's most popular heavy bands" and announcing "we join the show as Nazareth come on stage to perform 'Razamanaz,'" which is not true. The show opened with a glorious version of "Telegram"; they just didn't include it on radio. But "Razamanaz" does get a near-complete overhaul with both guitarists blazing throughout. Never before has this song sounded as unshackled as it does here. The energy is so intoxicating that McCafferty makes a mistake in the lyrics for the first line of the third verse, something that rarely happened with the dependable frontman. The newly-struck energy seems to have given Darrell Sweet an extra push as well. Simply put, his drumming on this track is the best it's ever been.

"I Want To Do Everything For You" begins with the axe team rolling out large sheets of sound, pulverizing the crowd, and ends with some tasty twin lead playing.

"Showdown At The Border" is much better in a live setting and has a middle guitar part that predicts AC/DC's "Thunderstruck" by ten years. Dan proclaims the band's work ethic, exclaiming, "This is no business for the weak at heart!"

During Dan's introduction of "Heart's Grown Cold," some punter in the crowd actually calls out for "Bad Boy." The guys attempt the gospel-ish backing vocals on the studio version, and Charlton and Cleminson play the brief guitar solo in unison.

"Big Boy" is toughened up with noisy guitar riffs and a nice bit of three-part harmony, during which an audience member exclaims,

"Awesome!" The track ends with Dan chanting, "What a night you can have," which is not on the studio recording.

"Holiday" is played more forcefully and with very dry lead vocals and then leads seamlessly into the galloping rhythm of "This Flight Tonight." Again, fiery axe work lifts the song to a new level of grandness. The near-medley of the two songs works well, and one wonders why this approach wasn't kept for future concerts.

It's no surprise that "Hair of the Dog" also benefits greatly from having the guitar riffs thickened by Cleminson's presence.

As expected, even a somewhat weaker track like "Talkin' To One Of The Boys" gets new life when essayed in an appreciative concert setting, proving that Nazareth should have road tested some of the *Malice* material before entering Compass Point Studios. This track also features both Charlton and Cleminson playing different guitar solos at the same time, leading to a cacophonous delight. The exuberance of playing the tune live is evidenced when McCafferty ends the song with an eardrum-shattering "All right!"

By "Expect No Mercy," Dan's vocals have achieved the proper amount of grit needed to deliver the intensity of this crowd favourite. Usually when introducing tunes in concert, McCafferty uses his lower speaking voice to enunciate the song title. Here, to kick off the song, he simply barks, "Expect no mercy!" to the assembled crowd.

The broadcast finishes with a stirring rendition of "Broken Down Angel," not least because of the exhilarated crowd singing the chorus a few times on their own before the band kicks back in to wrap things up.

This vibrant recording corrects the fairly conservative original setting treatment the *Malice* songs received while adding fresh layers to the older material with truly top-flight performances by the entire band. The Charlton-Cleminson twosome in particular fills every possible nook and cranny with as many power chords, frantic lead lines, and/or incessant soloing as humanly possible.

If released at the time as an official live album, Nazareth would have a career-defining work of awe-inspiring art that would stand proudly with the strongest pillars in the field (Thin Lizzy *Live And Dangerous*, AC/DC *If You Want Blood*, Blue Oyster Cult *Some Enchanted Evening*, and so on). If so, the upcoming downward trajectory of the band's fortunes surely would have been averted, or at least postponed for a few years.

RE-ISSUES, RE-MASTERS, AND RE-RECORDINGS

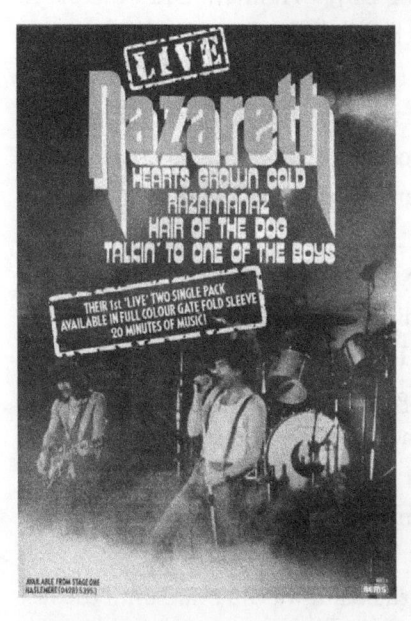

The first official release of any of the Hammersmith material came with the double seven-inch vinyl *Live* EP (BSD 1) featuring the songs "Razamanaz," "Heart's Grown Cold," "Talkin' To One Of The Boys," and "Hair of the Dog." This powerful release came in a terrific gatefold sleeve, the cover of which captured the band onstage in full flight under hot lights surrounded by billowing smoke.

When Castle released their 1998 reissue CD of the *Malice In Wonderland* album, they (wisely) included the four tracks that made up the *Live* EP as bonus material.

In 2001, the songs "Talkin' To One Of The Boys," "Broken Down Angel," "Heart's Grown Cold," and "Showdown At The Border" appeared on the two-CD live compilation *Back To The Trenches*.

The 2002 Eagle Records *Malice* CD adds single edits of "Holiday" and "Ship Of Dreams," although "Holiday" simply has an early fade, and "Ship Of Dreams" omits the middle bridge and instrumental breakdown. The circulating demo of "Big Boy" would have been a much more worthwhile bonus track than either of these fake constructions. It's exclusion is inexcusable.

Salvo's 2010 CD has eight different tracks from the Hammersmith show: "I Want To Do Everything For You," "Showdown At The Border," "Beggars Day," "Big Boy," "Holiday," "This Flight Tonight," "Expect No Mercy," and "Broken Down Angel." They all sound crisp and sharp to showcase the excellent performances. But if Salvo was just going to cherry pick various songs from the gig, they should have included all five of the *Malice* songs they played that night ("Showdown At The Border," "Heart's Grown Cold," "Big Boy," "Holiday," and "Talkin' To One Of The Boys"). In fact, they chose just two and then included a couple of faves like "Beggar's Day" (this version had not been released previously) and the "Holiday/This Flight Tonight" double shot. It would have made for a more interesting set of bonus tracks, as many of these tunes were not regular parts of the concert set list after the 1980 tour.

Even better would have been to make the *Malice* reissue a two-CD deluxe edition with the second disc comprised of as much of the Hammersmith show as possible. Issuing it in bits and pieces over years isn't doing anyone, including this lineup's legacy, any favours. At this late stage in the game, the lack of a full release of the complete 1980 Hammersmith show is a lost opportunity. Material this strong should not be relegated to supplemental material spread over various CD reissues.

A footnote to this album is that the band was unaware until the last moment that their then ex-Deep Purple friend Jon Lord had released an album with his new band PAL in March 1977 with the title *Malice in Wonderland*. Made up of Ian Paice (drums), Tony Ashton (vocals and keyboards), Bernie Marsden (guitar), and Paul Martinez (bass guitar), PAL were a bluesy, sometimes funky, hard rock combo that, unfortunately, broke up in May 1978 after playing a few select dates. Although it was too late for Nazareth to change their album title, they acknowledged Lord's group with a liner notes mention: "No malice intended, PAL."

In 1980, Dan made a guest appearance on the album *Exiled* by the group Mitchell/Cole Mysteries singing the song "Dreaming," a dramatic rock tune with building momentum and excellent lead vocals from McCafferty. "Dreaming" was released as a single in Germany with the album track "Inner Conflict" on the B-side. Also in 1980, a unique German compilation was produced, entitled *Pop Lions: Love Hurts* and was made up of "This Flight Tonight," "Freewheeler," "Madelaine," "Razamanaz," "Shanghai'd In Shanghai," "Love Hurts," "Night Woman," "Loved And Lost," "Whisky Drinkin' Woman," and "Vancouver Shakedown." Obviously, someone had fun programming each side to end with the companion tracks "Shanghai'd In Shanghai" and "Vancouver Shakedown."

In 1983, Blackfoot included an upbeat, if ham-fisted, cover of "Heart's Grown Cold" on their *Siogno* album.

The Fool Circle
1981

BACKGROUND

Amid rehearsals for their next album, band members were preoccupied with settling some lingering business affairs following the death of manager Bill Fehilly. This led to Zal Cleminson feeling increasing frustration that creating new music was not a priority. After weeks of this troubling distraction, he tendered his resignation. Some feel it was a blow from which Nazareth never fully recovered.

Eventually, the guys regrouped with producer Jeff "Skunk" Baxter on the Caribbean island of Montserrat and keyboardist John Locke of the American band Spirit sitting in on some of the sessions. Also along for the ride was acclaimed engineer Geoff Emerick, who had won Grammy awards for his work on the Beatles' *Sgt. Pepper's Lonely Hearts Club Band* (1967) and *Abbey Road* (1969) and would go on to helm Elvis Costello's 1982 masterpiece *Imperial Bedroom*.

When released in February 1981, *The Fool Circle* (NEL 6019) continued the soft rock approach of *Malice In Wonderland* but, surprisingly, revealed a more politically aware lyrical stance.

ALBUM OVERVIEW

The record opens with "Dressed To Kill," about the threat of nuclear annihilation at the hands of Russian politicians. It's a speedy rocker with robust piano, but the lack of any substantial guitar work renders it an inconsequential attempt. It's one of those tunes that needs a live airing to come into its own. "Another Year" is a politically-charged number that plods along until the chorus, which gives it a shot of adrenalin, although it's not enough to save the track. Salvaged from the aborted *Expect No Mercy* original sessions, a re-recording of "Moonlight Eyes" runs almost a minute longer and has a slightly quicker tempo with a bit more drumming and a sensitive vocal from McCafferty.

"Pop The Silo" has a bit of the rough and ready rumble of classic Nazareth. This anti-nuclear weapons rant begins with some sharp mandolin playing, a gurgling synthesizer just beneath the surface, and fragments of dialogue. A gentle reggae vibe permeates "Let Me Be Your Leader," featuring soft vocals, some delicate piano, and a dash of sweet acoustic guitar picking during the fadeout. An early Dire Straits feel is present on "We Are The People," showing just how much the band's style was changing.

"Every Young Man's Dream" is a harmless slice of pop confection with an odd synthesizer/guitar-sounding solo and some organ playing during the fade, adding some much-needed warmth to the album. The songwriting credit for this tune is attributed solely to drummer Darrell Sweet.

"Little Part Of You" is yet another poppy, commercial track with a tight rhythm that constricts Pete Agnew's playing, leaving him no room to move around. When you start to shackle an expressive a bass player like Agnew, you're heading for disappointment.

Recorded in Saginaw, Michigan on May 25, 1980, a live version of "Cocaine" follows. I'm not sure how it fits in with the album's convoluted political themes (okay, maybe it does, actually), but this worthwhile rendition is easily the best track on *The Fool Circle*. The mix is perfect, too. Pete's rumbling bass, Zal's resonating twelve-string acoustic, Manny's electric guitar, and Darrell's congas all sound clear and bright together. Dan's performance has a mischievousness wink to it, and even the crowd gets involved, singing along.

The album ends with the strange "Victoria," a buoyant cut that steals shamelessly from the Kinks' 1969 hit of the same name and also quotes the Beach Boys' 1964 single "Good Vibrations" at one point! Apparently, this is another Darrell Sweet solo contribution.

RELEASE AND RECEPTION

Once recording was finished, the band made a brief, five-song appearance on STV Scottish Television's *In Concert* program, filmed live at the Gateway Theatre in Edinburgh on December 17, 1980. This show was designed to introduce the group's two new official members, John Locke and Glaswegian guitarist Billy Rankin, to the world at large. (Rankin joined after the album was complete.)

The mini-set consists of a jubilant "Razamanaz," "I Want To Do Everything For You" (both with noticeable piano contributions from Locke), "Heart's Grown Cold" (with Rankin on twelve-string acoustic guitar), and a preview from the upcoming album, "Dressed To Kill," which Dan introduces with the "uplifting" thought, "We're gonna leave you with a song about how you're all going to die in World War Three." The seriousness of the subject matter is balanced a bit by the sight of Rankin doing a Chuck Berry duck walk across the small stage. Although brief, the footage is fantastic, with many close-ups of the guys, especially Dan, who is sporting a Lynyrd Skynyrd T-shirt. The show was broadcast at the end of January 1981.

The Fool Circle charted at twenty-nine in Norway, thirty-three in Sweden, sixty in the UK, seventy in the US, and thirty-one in Canada, where it earned the guys yet another gold album certification. Numerous international singles were released to promote the album in various territories. "Dressed To Kill," paired with "Pop The Silo" (NES 301), was issued in the UK, Spain, and Italy. "Every Young Man's Dream" with "Let Me Be Your Leader" on the B-side and "Moonlight Eyes" and "Pop The Silo" came out in Germany. "Let Me Be Your Leader" along with "Little Part Of You" was issued in Holland, "Let Me Be Your Leader" with "Victoria" on the flip side came out in Australia, "Victoria" and "We Are The People" was released in Spain, and a live version of "Cocaine" was paired with "Pop The Silo" in the Philippines.

Naturally, extensive touring continued, this time with opening act Krokus. (Although six of the ten songs, "Another Year," "Moonlight Eyes," "Pop The Silo," We Are The People," "Little Part Of You" and "Victoria" were never performed live.)

The tour included an important show in Vancouver on May 28, 1981, which longtime fan Ian Naismyth attended. "I was twenty something, stoned, at a Naz concert. Though I knew the guys from Dunfermline, I had moved recently from there to Vancouver and had not really reconnected with them. I did go back stage and managed to bump into Dan, but big, burly bouncers removed me immediately. All Dan had time to say was, 'What the feck are you doin' here?'

"I do recall that when they started to play 'Big Boy,' some chick threw a massive dong onstage, which Dan, without missing a beat, picked up and tucked into his waistband and kept singing with his new appendage dangling there. It was pretty funny."

If this wasn't enough Nazareth product for hungry fans, on August 7 the double vinyl soundtrack to the Canadian animated film *Heavy Metal* came out, featuring new tracks from Blue Oyster Cult, Cheap Trick, Black Sabbath, Sammy Hagar, and more. Nazareth is represented on this excellent compilation with a bloodthirsty new song "Crazy (A Suitable Case For Treatment)." The ambitious track begins with a stuttering acoustic that is steamrolled immediately by a hefty guitar riff. Anticipating a deteriorating and fragile mental state through its various movements, the bridge has some deep, uneasy vocals and a deceitfully simple piano solo that leads the listener further down the rabbit hole.

"Crazy (A Suitable Case For Treatment)" marked Billy Rankin's debut studio recording as a member of the band. The *Heavy Metal* soundtrack reached number twelve on the US charts.

Also released in 1981 was *Live And Heavy* (NEL 6020) on Nems Records, a compilation of tracks recorded in concert by groups like Deep Purple, Motorhead, Rainbow, Gillan, and others. Nazareth is represented by a scorching run-through "Razamanaz" taped at London's Hammersmith Odeon.

RE-ISSUES, RE-MASTERS, AND RE-RECORDINGS

The 1998 Castle CD of *The Fool Circle* has four bonus tracks that are simply the songs taken off Castle's CD release of the upcoming live album *Snaz*.

The 2002 Eagle Records release has fake single edits of "Dressed To Kill" (which inexplicably actually runs longer than the album version) and "Pop The Silo."

Salvo's 2010 CD has a total of six bonus tracks: "Morgantau," the German-sung version of "Morning Dew," "Crazy (A Suitable Case For Treatment)" from the *Heavy Metal* soundtrack, and the four songs found originally on the heroic *Live* EP, "Razamanaz," "Heart's Grown Cold," "Talkin' To One Of The Boys," and "Hair of the Dog" (although not in the original running order of the EP). The combination of the song "Crazy" with the *Live* EP packs a punch, making Salvo's *The Fool Circle* reissue easily the most worthwhile version.

Snaz
1981

BACKGROUND

During the band's *The Fool Circle* tour, multiple gigs in the US and Canada were recorded for consideration to be released as an official live album. Recorded on May 23, 1981 at the Pacific Coliseum in Vancouver, *Snaz* would be that album.

ALBUM OVERVIEW

"Telegram" sets the tone for the show, an authoritative, commanding introduction designed to captivate an arena filled with a self-medicated, denim-clad legion of followers. Next, Dan introduces "Razamanaz" with, "This is one you may remember," before the band tears into the song at full tilt. "I Want To Do Everything For You" opens with guitars crashing like waves while Darrell underpins the proceedings with authority. The song ends with some sinewy twin leads from Charlton and Rankin. "This Flight Tonight" includes some maudlin and completely unnecessary piano tinkling, although Dan is in fine form, as usual, rescuing the track. Speaking of which, for "Beggar's Day," he screams the chorus with an unbridled intensity that could shatter glass.

"Every Young Man's Dream" boasts an agreeable guitar figure and some funky bass playing along with an infectious chorus.

"Heart's Grown Cold" has an acoustic guitar and piano introduction that plays a few extra bars longer than on the original studio recording before the excellent lead vocals kick in. At that point, Dan introduces the two new members of the group, and then they jump right into a rollicking take on Rick Danko's "Java Blues" from his 1977 self-titled solo album.

A tribute to a slightly stronger stimulant than coffee, the next song, written by J. J. Cale, is "Cocaine," beginning with some acoustic guitar playing from Rankin. "Big Boy" benefits from pounding riffs and a tremendous vocal from Dan, who plays around with some of his phrasing. His vocals elevate the track into the status of "live classic." The Vancouver recording of "Big Boy" is actually one of the few songs (maybe the only one) that sound heavier on *Snaz* than when performed by the Zal Cleminson lineup "Holiday" accentuates the track's forward motion and has near perfect vocal harmonies.

An extra boost to the drums on "Dressed To Kill" helps to move it forward. A ringing cowbell announces "Hair of the Dog" before Charlton unleashes the famous, king-sized guitar riff. Dan encourages some enthusiastic crowd participation. What Canadian teenager wouldn't jump at the chance to break national character and scream "Son of a bitch!" at the top of his or her weed-filled lungs?

Some tentative guitar shapes are thrown around the hall before the pile-driving "Expect No Mercy" riff is launched to the far corners of the arena.

A live highlight, "Shapes Of Things" features Dan's unholy, echo-laden screech penetrating eardrums everywhere. The spacey excursion in the middle gives the crowd a few minutes to catch their collective breath before McCafferty barks "Shapes!" to snap the thundering track back into focus.

"Let Me Be Your Leader" actually begins with some huge, Black Sabbath-style guitar carvings before settling into the laid-back reggae groove.

Faithful to the original, "Love Hurts" no doubt caused a sea of flickering cigarette lighters to rise up from the arena floor. Dan gives a delicate vocal performance, wrapping his distinctive rasp around every lyric.

The show ends with a battery-charged cover of ZZ Top's "Tush" with honky-tonk piano, a sparse, bluesy guitar solo, and McCafferty's surprisingly still functioning larynx. John Locke's decision to switch from piano to a bright synthesizer halfway through the song for the solo probably should have been given a second thought, as it does not fit with the sun-parched Texas vibe. After the solo, he goes back to the piano and then inexplicably returns to the synth for the end of the track.

In addition to the eighteen-song live set that comprises the majority of *Snaz*, listeners are also treated to two brand new studio recordings.

A steady backbeat propels "Juicy Lucy," a little rocker with a slight southern accent from Dan. Charlton ends the song with a solo that combines searing held notes and frenetic shredding. Also included is a redundant re-recording of Bonnie Dobson's "Morning Dew" (henceforth to be referred to herein as "Morning Dew '81") with a vaguely disco beat. Did *Snaz* really need additional material this badly? The re-recording adds nothing to the good work done on the band's original 1971 version.

RELEASE AND RECEPTION

September 1981 saw the release of *Snaz*, (NELD 102), the band's first double live set. The album hit number eighty-three in the US and number seventy-eight in the UK.

Singles released to help promote the album were: "Morning Dew '81" with "Juicy Lucy" on the B-side (NES 302) in the UK and Germany, "Morning Dew '81" and "Love Hurts (live)" in France, and "Love Hurts" (live) and "Holiday" (live) in Holland. A&M Records released a twelve-inch sampler *Selections From Snaz* (SP-17175) in North America. It consisted of "Morning Dew '81," "Love Hurts," "Hair of the Dog," "Juicy Lucy," "Dressed To Kill," and "Holiday." The original German vinyl release included a free, one-sided "Morgentau" single (6843029) on the Vertigo label. The South Korean version (SEL RP 1092) used a shot of the empty stage from a packed concert.

Having a new live career retrospective release didn't mean the guys were going to take it easy. They continued touring, including a show at the Apollo in Glasgow on September 20, 1981, home to definitive live albums by AC/DC (*If You Want Blood You've Got It*) and Rush (*Exit Stage Left*). Home field advantage is clear, as the guys are in top form. In fact, Darrell Sweet delivers some of his strongest drumming to date, and John Locke alternates between electric piano and synthesizer for these live tracks.

In the US, the band continued to tour, this time with opening act the Joe Perry Project, who were promoting their exceptional second album *I've Got The Rock 'n' Rolls Again*.

Another consequential show on the tour occurred at the Sam Houston Coliseum in Houston on November 28, 1981, which, thankfully, was caught on film. (At one point early in the film, a venue marquee is seen displaying the concert date as May 7 with openers Trapeze and Krokus.) Playing a set list similar to the one that makes up *Snaz* (the film is clearly not the full show) makes for a valuable visual companion to the double LP. It's nice to see Charlton and Rankin engage in some dual lead playing, as they do at the end of "Dressed To Kill." Before "Cocaine," Dan asks the crowd if they want to be on a record, which is strange, because at that point the album was already out. Maybe Dan thought that since they had two albums in a row with live versions of the song, why not go for a hat trick? In a quick cutaway during "Hair of the Dog," we learn that a roadie is playing the infamous cowbell part while "Shapes Of Things" explodes in a cloud of smoke and brimstone.

Interspersed among the exciting live footage are scenes of the guys on their tour bus, backstage, and walking around what appears to be New Orleans. Also included is a scene of John Locke writing out the set list, but we have to assume he's just making copies of what Dan or Pete have decided and is not actually choosing the program for the evening.

Overall, the quality of the film is darker than anyone would prefer.

RE-ISSUES, RE-MASTERS, AND RE-RECORDINGS

Four songs from the riotous September 20, 1981 gig, "Hair of the Dog," "Expect No Mercy," "Love Hurts," and "Shapes Of Things," were released on the 2001 two-CD compilation *Back To The Trenches: Live 1972–1984*. However, some problematic releases from this period have also surfaced over the years.

The November 28, 1981 Houston footage was released unofficially on DVD in 2005 as *Live In Texas* by River Records and in 2007 as *Hair of the Dog Live* by Cleopatra Records.

A 2004 CD by River Records, with the meaningless title *The River Sessions*, begins with six songs from the September 20, 1981 Glasgow concert and then switches to nine songs from the Houston video. A noticeable drop in sound quality betrays the Houston shows' VHS source. The continuity of a live show would at least have been implied if the two sections were swapped. Anyone with a basic knowledge of Nazareth's 1970s set lists will be dismayed to see "Telegram" performed as the seventh song. In the film, "I Want To Do Everything For You" fades before the vocals even start to show footage of the band offstage. Inexplicably, *The River Sessions*, which calls the song "Do Everything," replicates this early fade out. The next song, "Holiday," has a bit of an early fade as well with crowd noise brought up way too high in the mix.

In 2007, Cleopatra Records issued a bootleg of *The River Sessions*, entitled *Hair of the Dog Live*, which is exactly the same recording just with different (read: awful) cover artwork.

What's really a shame about these releases is that, if done competently, they would be extremely valuable additions to any rock fan's collection. The Houston footage should be made available in a re-mastered home video format, and the complete Glasgow recording would be a worthwhile aural snapshot of this era of the band's history. The lack of care in these releases is unfortunate considering how appreciable the playing is.

If you think fans were treated unkindly by the producers of these substandard titles, one supporter was ripped off artistically as well. Jon

Hahn tells his story: "On November 4, 1983, I saw Nazareth in a classy place called the Brandywine Club in Chadds Ford, PA. I saw a bunch of great bands there in the early eighties, and it was one of my favorite places to see shows, since they were open to allowing people to take photographs, and I was into taking concert shots back then as a hobby. I had an 'advanced' 35mm SLR camera at the time called a Canon AE-1 (still have it today), and through many gigs, I learned how to use it get good concert photos (i.e., never use a flash, and try to get shots that give a feel for the show, capturing those special moments in time where something is 'happening.') You might have to burn three rolls of film to get just one special shot, but keep at it, and you'll get something worthwhile by the end of the night.

"Eventually, the song 'Hair of the Dog' got an airing, and in there they played a section of 'The Bonnie Banks o' Loch Lomond' ('you take the high road and I'll take the low road') with Manny using a talkbox thing like Peter Frampton, which was routed into a set of bagpipes that Dan was holding. Second guitarist Billy Rankin (with his Scottish tartan guitar) started clowning around next to Dan while Dan was 'playing' the bagpipes during this and—Presto! With camera in hand and snapping shots as fast as I could advance the film with one hand and hit the shoot button with the other, I captured a magical moment in time, getting about a half dozen photos in sequence of the two of them goofing around.

"I used to have a website, and I set up a photo section on there with some of my favorite concert shots for others to enjoy. On my index page I stated, 'If you would like to use these for yourself, please feel free to do so on the condition that you do not alter them in any way, do not sell them, and that you mention where you got them from. Thanks.'

"Having that stuff on the 'net led me to hear from some interesting people, including many of the musicians I photographed, and that was pretty cool. Some people asked for permission to use my photos, and I rarely said no and never asked for anything in return. Over the years, I've seen some of my photos appear in really strange places without my permission. People have used them for forum avatars, sold some of them as buttons on eBay, all kinds of weird stuff, but I always looked on that as an honor that anyone would like them enough to want to use them, even if I got no credit per se.

"Until a few years ago, I never stumbled across any of my photos in an album release without being asked permission, and then I saw one of the shots I took of Nazareth at the Brandywine of Billy clowning next to Dan in the Nazareth release entitled *The River Sessions*. I couldn't believe it! No mention of where the shot was from, no info at all. Very strange. I would think that someone releasing an album for sale would only use images they got from sources that had okayed their use, but I don't mind. That I was lucky enough to capture that magical moment and now even more people get to see it on an actual album is kind of cool." (Jon's photo also appears on the back cover of the *Hair of the Dog Live* DVD.)

To fit *Snaz* onto a single CD, the 1997 Castle release omits "Every Young Man's Dream," "Big Boy" (the edit where "Big Boy" is supposed to start is very noticeable), and the two studio tracks.

Eagle Records' 2002 release has an alternate edit of "Juicy Lucy," which is a fake bonus track that is all of three seconds shorter than the album take, rendering it useless even as a fake oddity.

The 2011 Salvo release is one of the better titles in this label's reissue series. Finally, a two-CD set! Not only does the Salvo version of *Snaz* present the complete material found on the original vinyl on CD for the first time, it also includes some top-notch bonus material.

First, we are presented with seven tracks from a 1981 show in Seattle. Considering that this recording is from a gig soon after the Vancouver show, it's not surprising that there aren't any major differences in the performances. Two examples: McCafferty breaks character and laughs during the chorus to "Bad Boy," and Rankin's guitar solo on "Holiday" has an extra layer of noisy distortion. Even without major performance differences, the sound quality is stunning (clearer than *Snaz*, actually), making this material invaluable for the faithful.

Other supplemental material on the Salvo deluxe edition are the tracks "Morgentau" (the regrettable German version of "Morning Dew") and "Crazy (A Suitable Case For Treatment)" from the *Heavy Metal* soundtrack.

A circulating recording known in collectors' circles as *Raw Snaz* is the original May 23, 1981 Vancouver tape before any post-production cleanup work was done to prepare the show for official release as *Snaz*. As expected, elements of between-song patter were removed from the finished album. Dialogue after "Telegram," "I Want To Do Everything For You" (about the show being recorded for a live album), "Heart's Grown Cold," and "Cocaine" (a fitting tribute to the road crew) were all edited, as was some talk before "Every Young Man's Dream."

What is most revealing, however, is that if *Raw Snaz* truly is the complete May 23 Vancouver show (and it includes enough mentions of the city to confirm that it is), then *Snaz* itself is actually a pastiche of different shows (Calgary has been suggested as a possibility) edited together to appear as a singe concert. The version of "Big Boy" on *Snaz*, for example, is obviously not from the Vancouver show (and Dan's laugh during the *Raw Snaz* version might substantiate Ian Naismyth's account of a sex toy being thrown to the singer during the song). Then again, the versions of "Tush" on *Snaz* and *Raw Snaz* both have Dan thanking Vancouver yet are obviously two different performances of the song. Fans who were present confirm that two shows did not take place in Vancouver on that tour, so the source for the different "Tush" recording remains a mystery.

This isn't really an issue though, because many of the greatest live albums of all time were put together similarly from numerous concerts and have additional studio work done. But fans have been told that *Snaz* is from that particular Vancouver show for so long that the examination of *Raw Snaz* is startling for what it reveals. For fans of *Snaz*, *Raw Snaz* is essential listening and, in fact, more than deserves an official release.

2XS
1983

BACKGROUND

With the more laid-back releases *Malice in Wonderland* and *The Fool Circle* plus the tour to promote *Snaz* behind them, Nazareth stood on the precipice looking towards an uncertain future. Would they work to reclaim the hard rock status that had cemented their reputation or continue with the more recent, pop-friendly material that had comprised their latest releases?

In the summer of 1982, fans got their collective answer with the release of *2XS* (NIN 001), the band's fourth release to be comprised completely of original material. (In retrospect, should have attempted a couple of covers.) Recorded at Air Studios in Montserrat and produced by John Pinter, the new album served to be divisive within fan circles.

ALBUM OVERVIEW

The record opens promisingly with "Love Leads To Madness," which has banks of acoustic guitars and a tasty electric lead on top. This is a perfect example of Nazareth constructing a radio-friendly tune without sacrificing their identity. All of the Nazareth trademarks are there, notably Dan's expressive growl and Manny's fluid lead guitar playing.

Things proceed well with "Boys In The Band," a nonstop raver in the vein of "Teenage Nervous Breakdown" that has a strong piano solo over some synthesizer shadings. However, "You Love Another" has horribly dated drum machine programming, which derails the track despite an impassioned McCafferty lead vocal (with howling backing vocals) and decent guitar playing.

Things get moving again with "Gatecrash," a rockabilly rave with multiple acoustic guitars providing the foundation. The piano solo is suitably late-1950s sounding, and the track ends with a sustaining note of guitar feedback that leads directly into the next cut, "Games." This is another tune with a drum machine dragging the beat, although is also includes some light acoustic guitar picking and a soft McCafferty vocal that expands into a barrel-chested declaration of independence or triumph or something.

A street-tough rocker with a snarling lead vocal, "Back To The Trenches" goes a long way towards getting things in order again. More of this is desperately required.

The sensitive ballad "Dream On" has acoustic guitar, piano, and rising synths plus a yearning lead vocal. One can practically feel the light being reflected from a slowly spinning glitter ball during this soon-to-be prom slow dance standard. Although credited to the entire band, "Dream On" is actually a Billy Rankin composition. Rankin's original 1979 demo is nearly identical in terms of arrangement and lyrical content to the finished Nazareth rendition.

An example of pure 1980s keyboard pop, "Lonely In The Night" bounces along at a quick clip as if the musicians can't wait to get the thing over and done with. Who could blame them?

"Preservation" has awful, plastic-sounding keyboards and synth drums that kill whatever chance this lifeless skeleton might have had.

A fast, little rocker, "Take The Rap" has some good guitar riffing, handclaps, bright piano, and (thankfully) real drums, which could still be a bit higher in the mix. Usually, this sort of thing wouldn't stand out as anything too noteworthy, but against the backdrop of the other tracks on 2XS, it's a pillar of greatness.

The album wraps things up with "Mexico," a synth-heavy attempt with multiple acoustic guitars and a laid-back vocal from McCafferty.

When all is said and done, out of the eleven tracks, a little more than half are in the "passable" to "good" category (I know, I'm being generous), meaning that there's an okay EP within the album, and you don't have to look too hard to find it.

RELEASE AND RECEPTION

Riding the vapour trails of the previous decade's successes, 2XS reached number nine in Norway, number forty-two in Germany, number seventy-four in Canada, and number one hundred and twenty-two in the US. Multiple singles worked hard to get those chart numbers.

"Love Leads To Madness," paired with "Take The Rap" (NIS 101), reached number three in South Africa, number nineteen in the US, and number forty-four in Canada. (It was also released in the UK, Germany, Holland, Brazil, and France.) "Games" with "You Love Another" on the B-side (NIS 102) failed to chart, but the pairing of "Dream On" and "Juicy Lucy" (NIS 103) was a hit in Switzerland, where it achieved a number two chart position; Austria, where it was number four; and Germany, where it was number fifteen. (It was also released in the UK, France, and Holland.) "Dream On," paired with "Games," was a non-charting single in Spain, while "Dream On" with the B-side "You Love Another" came out in Germany. In France, a twelve-inch, three-track single consisted of "Dream On," "Preservation," and "Love Leads To Madness."

A&M Records released a seven-inch promotional single (2421) in the US consisting of mono and stereo versions of "Love Leads To Madness." A seven-inch four-track was released in Brazil (6200 038), consisting of "Love Hurts," "I Don't Want To Go On Without You," "Hair of the Dog," and "Shot Me Down."

An unfortunate music video for "Dream On" was lensed with a sci-fi concept that has the group as space explorers, a obvious conceptual misstep for such a heartfelt and grounded ballad. The tracks "You Love Another," "Games," "Lonely In The Night," "Take The Rap," and "Mexico" have never been performed live by the group.

On February 14, 1983, Nazareth played a charity concert at Coasters (a.k.a. Coasters Roller Disco) in Tollcross, Edinburgh. The excellent, fifteen-song radio broadcast of this intimate gig features no less than five cuts from the new album: "Boys In The Band," "Love Leads To Madness," "Dream On," "Gatecrash," and "Back To The Trenches." All of the tracks are improved upon greatly when heard live, and an extra bonus is hearing Dan's actual speaking voice when introducing various numbers. (He softens his accent when performing abroad.) In addition to being broadcast over the radio, some parts of this concert were filmed for German television.

Longtime fan Michael Tasker was at the Coasters gig. "This was a big occasion. Nazareth had not been in town since September 1981 for the *Snaz* tour. The packed Odeon theatre that night had witnessed a blistering performance of a rock band in top form that would rank amongst their best gigs in Edinburgh.

"Coasters was, at the time, a roller skating music club that hosted rock shows on occasion. Naz had teamed up with local radio station Radio Forth to raise money for charity, and the show was recorded and subsequently broadcast by the station. A German TV crew also filmed the show. No pressure then . . . .

"The show was also one of the first that the band played after reverting to a five-piece with the departure of John Locke back to his band Spirit. Back to the raw two guitars of the Zal years. The sound check (I had been invited to watch by Willie McQuillan, the band's longtime crew member) confirmed that Naz was louder and tighter than ever, storming their way through 'Beggars Day' and 'Back to the Trenches.'

"The venue was packed with one thousand fans crammed in, and I mean crammed in. It was hot, and the crowd was high, waiting to welcome a band they knew would rock the place to its foundations. The set list was sprinkled with a few songs from the recently-released *2XS* album, with 'Love Leads To Madness,' a great sing-along tune, the head-banging brilliance of 'Boys In The Band,' and the mean and meaty 'Back To The Trenches.' It wouldn't be Naz without the obligatory ballad, and hearing 'Dream On' live for the first time was magical. It had all the hallmarks of being a Naz classic.

"The show was finished off with an encore that was sheer bedlam. A tidal wave of sound engulfed the adoring crowd as the pumping 'Morning Dew' took no prisoners, and then, for an artistic interlude, Manny gave a partial rendition of 'The Dance' from the Nutcracker Suite, where the crowd found a last few breaths to sing along until we were all pinned back by the sheer tsunami of guitar sound that introduced 'Tush.'

"Naz was back in town, a thundering statement was made, and the lasting impression was that we were fortunate to be present for one of those rare evenings where you can get up close and party with your favourite rockers."

In May, the band rejoined their old touring mates Rush for a series of dates in Germany. Rush was on the road promoting their current album, *Signals*.

Just before the release of their next album in October, Nazareth played four shows in Canada, opening for Black Sabbath (fronted by their old friend Ian Gillan), who were touring the underrated *Born Again* album. After shows in Quebec City (October 20), Montreal (October 21), Ottawa (October 22) and Sudbury (October 24), Nazareth actually replaced Sabbath at the October 26 show in London, Ontario when the headliners cancelled at the last minute.

RE-ISSUES, RE-MASTERS, AND RE-RECORDINGS

Portions of one of the shows on the *2XS* tour were released on the essential 2001 archival release *Back To The Trenches Live 1972–1984*.

Seven songs from the gig in Fort Pierce, Florida on September 12, 1982 capture this era of the group's history with encouraging results, since five of the seven tracks are from the new album but are recast as the heavy slabs to which fans are accustomed.

Opening track "Boys In The Band" has Dan in full-on, reptilian glory and a piano buried under thick wall of guitars. Next up are perfectly fine renditions of "Beggar's Day" and "This Flight Tonight" before we are ushered into a quartet of reimagined 2XS material and are all the better for it.

Also included is a solid, if a bit heavy-handed, replication of the studio version of "Love Leads To Madness," where it's nice to hear Darrell Sweet get in some extra licks. "Gatecrash" retains its late-1950s rockabilly feel, although the electric piano solo takes the listener out of the vibe. The unimpressive album track, "Preservation," gets new life in the live setting as the guitars get dirtied up and Dan does his best to add a malevolent edge to his vocal.

It's not surprising that "Back To The Trenches," which was actually decent in its studio incarnation, is even better when performed in front of an appreciative crowd. Extra-hard riffing and a totally engaged Sweet drive this one home with integrity.

The 1999 Castle CD sports six bonus tracks: "Dream On" (single edit), "Juicy Lucy" (alternate edit), "Games" (alternate edit), "You Love Another" (alternate edit), "Love Leads To Madness" (alternate single version), and "Dream On" (mono mix).

The "Dream On" (single edit) and "Games" (alternate edit) are only marginally different than the album versions, while the "You Love Another" (alternate edit) and "Love Leads To Madness" (alternate single version) merely fade early.

The 2002 Eagle Records CD has five of the Castle bonus tracks (sensibly omitting "Juicy Lucy") and extended versions of "Back To The Trenches" and "Love Leads To Madness." Both of these are fake bonus cuts. "Back To The Trenches" repeats the first verse while "Love Leads To Madness" repeats all three verses twice to pad out the running time.

The 2011 Salvo CD combines 2XS with the follow-up album *Sound Elixir*, leaving no room for bonus tracks, real or faked, but the four-CD boxed set *The Naz Box* (also released in 2011) does include a rare demo of the song "Mexico." This raw take has more pronounced acoustic guitars, a slightly muffled lead vocal, and, most interestingly, the second and third verses of the album track are missing and simply replaced with the first verse repeated in their place. This genuine rarity should have replaced one of the fake bonus tracks on the Castle and/or Eagle Records CDs.

In terms of covers, Canadian metal band Helix recorded a pretty faithful version of "Dream On" on their 1987 *Wild in the Streets* album.

Sound Elixir
1983

BACKGROUND

If *2XS* was met with an element of confusion on the part of the record-buying public, the follow-up, *Sound Elixir*, caused hard rock fans to recoil in horror. Any remnants of the group's proven hard rock sensibilities were jettisoned in favour of stiff, over-produced arrangements lacking any shred of humanity. Where returning to a metallic aesthetic could have lent a sense of forgiveness to *2XS* as an anomaly, *Sound Elixir* actually elevates the former release to a status far above its minimal accomplishments. That's not an easy trick to pull off.

Recorded at Little Mountain Studios in Vancouver, Canada, and seeing guitarist Manny Charlton return to the production chair should have been an instant recipe for success. It wasn't.

ALBUM OVERVIEW

Sound Elixir opens with "All Night Radio," featuring mandolin (interesting) and synth-drums (far from interesting) and is notable for the band's first use of prevalent backwards guitar. (Some is heard on "Boys In The Band" from the previous album, but it's not as up front as it is here.)

"Milk & Honey" has swelling synthesizers, a strutting Pete Agnew bass guitar, Beach Boys-style harmonies on the chorus, and a lead vocal that is inexplicably distant in the mix. At least the sentiment of "Milk & Honey" is decent enough, chastising the American exploitation of Native Indians. Some good, hard guitar riffing and solid drums give "Whippin' Boy" an acceptably heavy groove, but it is almost undermined by the unnecessarily processed gang vocals on the chorus. The frantic, if brief, guitar solo helps out as well.

"Rain On The Window" has a slight country feel to it with acoustic picking and a comforting lyric. It also has a synthesizer solo courtesy of guitarist Billy Rankin that sounds completely out of place. Ironically, a gentle approach to this song probably would have been more suitable.

Marred by harsh percussion, at least "Backroom Boys" has some mandolin playing and a little more push in McCafferty's vocals. A nicely-played guitar solo is about all "Why Don't You Read The Book" has going for it, with the two-finger keyboard hammering supported by an angular guitar figure setting the listener up for distraction.

"I Ran" has a slightly funky undercurrent, as if that's enough to intrigue the listener to spend time with the track (it isn't). Overall, it's such a smooth piece with none of the grit for which the band is known that it's actually hard to believe this isn't a Jeff "Skunk" Baxter production job. It's these kinds of aesthetic decisions that make *Sound Elixir* a flat and tasteless aural brew.

"Rags To Riches" is an uplifting, fist-in-the-air anthem designed to accompany some kind of "triumph over adversity" narrative. At least that's what it sounds like they were going for.

Next is "Local Still," a slightly Celtic romp with a mandolin barely audible in the mix.

The album ends with "Where Are You Now," a piano-led, mid-tempo ballad with some backwards guitar and a strong lead vocal.

Other songs demoed during the sessions include "Baby's Got A Gun," an impatient, little speedster with a clean guitar solo and high backing vocals; "Blue Sky," a cheery slice of melodic pop with great lead vocals; and "Let Me See The Light," which, although a low-fi recording, boasts a memorable, ready-for-radio chorus. Also reportedly from this era is "Crime And Punishment Show," a rumbling march with a lean guitar solo during the fade out.

Photo: John Hahn Nov 4 1983

RELEASE AND RECEPTION

"Where Are You Now," backed with the previously-unreleased "On The Run," was released as a single in Holland, Germany, Brazil, and the Philippines. A music video for the track has Dan pining for the girl of his dreams while the band strums along. Additionally, the guys appeared on European TV lip-synching to "Where Are You Now" with Billy Rankin seated at a grand piano.

At a January 1984 show in Providence, Rhode Island, the band opened with a strong version of "All Nite Radio," featuring a heavy, lumbering groove delivered with authority and a sense of purpose.

"Beggar's Day" is delivered with excellent lead vocals from McCafferty and has some extra lead guitar playing added to the arrangement. During "Whippin' Boy," Dan's vocal seems to have an extra layer of menace, and that's saying something.

A high-energy rendition of "Boys In The Band" is followed by an aggressive version of "Expect No Mercy," proving that as commercial sounding as the recent two albums were, the band was still a down and dirty live unit.

The songs "Milk And Honey," "Rain On The Window," "Why Don't You Read The Book," "I Ran," and "Rags To Riches" have never been played live by the band.

How out of touch was Nazareth at this time? Well, consider that the year they released both *2XS* and *Sound Elixir*, their softest records to day, the following albums were also new in the shops: Def Leppard's *Pyromania*, Quiet Riot's *Metal Health*, and *Shout At The Devil* by Motley Crue. If keeping up with the new crop of metal bands seemed like too much for them, numerous hard rock bands who had also been around for years were still releasing quality product. Examples include AC/DC's *Flick Of The Switch*, Black Sabbath's *Born Again*, Dio's *Holy Diver*, *Lick It Up* by Kiss, Thin Lizzy's *Thunder And Lightning*, and Ozzy Osbourne's *Bark At The Moon*. Some older, non-hard rock artists who were also proving their relevance in 1983 include David Bowie with *Let's Dance*, Robert Plant with *The Principle Of Moments*, the Rolling Stones with *Undercover*, and even Nazareth pals ZZ Top, who scored big with *Eliminator*. If Nazareth had delivered a halfway heavier album than either *2XS* or *Sound Elixir* and were able to get a supporting gig touring with any of the artists mentioned previously, history would have turned out much differently for the Scottish rockers.

In their defense (sort of), they weren't the only 1970s heritage act who had a difficult go at adapting to the times. After all, Alice Cooper released the unlistenable *Da Da* album in 1983.

Out of the group in 1983, Billy Rankin kept busy with a solo album, *Growin' Up Too Fast* (1984), which featured the surprise US hit single "Baby Come Back," which reached number fifty-two. The album, released on A&M Records, also had a re-recording of the *Sound Elixir* track "Where Are You Now" and and outtake from that album, "Baby's Got A Gun."

RE-ISSUES, RE-MASTERS, AND RE-RECORDINGS

In 1989, MCA Records re-released a radical new version of *Sound Elixir* on cassette in the US. Retitled *All Nite Radio,* this eight-song tape omits "Backroom Boys" and "Local Still" and also changes the running order of the remaining material. The cassette's cover is a portrait of the band rather than the established and memorable *Sound Elixir* photo of a crate of moonshine bottles.

Three tracks from the *Sound Elixir* tour stop at the Commodore Ballroom in Vancouver on October 1, 1983 appeared on the *Back to the Trenches Live 1972–1984* two-CD set. Persistent sequencers throb through "All Nite Radio" in its live arrangement, but at least Darrell has a more approachable drum sound than on the record. "Razamanaz" is performed with the expected zest, and "Whippin' Boy" gets a swinging rhythm that elevates the live cut of this tune, which was already one of the few rockin' tracks on the studio album. A full hour of this Vancouver show was broadcast on 99.3 The Fox radio and is an outstanding document from the *Sound Elixir* tour. The complete broadcast is release-worthy.

The 1999 Castle CD comes with three bonus tracks: "On The Run," "Where Are You Now" (alternate edit) and "Milk & Honey" (alternate edit). The B-side, "On The Run," is a respectable track that, had it replaced a weaker number like "Backroom Boys," "Why Don't You Read The Book," or "I Ran," would have helped the album overall. That's not to say it's an exceptional song, which it isn't, but it is better than almost half of what made it onto the record. The alternate edit of

"Where Are You Now" is completely fake, awkwardly repeating the first verse after the guitar solo, while the "Milk & Honey" alternate edit just drags on a bit longer (how a longer version can be considered an "edit" is a mystery). For some reason, the Castle CD has a blurry and overall poor reproduction of the original vinyl record sleeve as the booklet cover.

The 2002 Eagle Records CD has the two "alternate edits" from the Castle release plus a radio edit of "All Nite Radio" (cropping the intro) and an extended version of "Whippin' Boy" that repeats the beginning guitar figure for a few extra bars before the vocals come in. Instead of padding the running time with fake alternate edits, Billy Rankin's excellent original demo of "Whippin' Boy" is a fully-realized and release-worthy rendition that should have been included as a bonus track.

As mentioned previously, the 2011 Salvo release presents both *2XS* and *Sound Elixir* on a single CD, leaving no room for bonus tracks. However, the 2011 four-CD boxed set, *The Naz Box*, does not ignore this period at all, presenting three studio outtakes from *Sound Elixir*. "Laid To Wasted" has acoustic guitars, real drums(!), and an expressive electric guitar solo and should have at least been a bonus track on the Castle CD reissue. A tune with this much heart simply should not have been cast aside.

"Read The Book" is a decent track with an unobtrusive wash of synthesizers. It is not to be confused with the similarly titled album track "Why Don't You Read The Book," as they are completely different compositions. Finally, "SOS" has a dark keyboard throb and electronic drums that give a slightly menacing feel while Dan bemoans the end of a relationship. Even with Dan pleading, "When you're gone, how can I even try to go on," it's obvious that this is the bleakest cover of an Abba song ever heard by mortal ears.

The Catch
1984–1985

BACKGROUND

In 1984, Nazareth's Canadian label, A&M Records, released a double LP compilation, *The Very Very Best Of Nazareth* (SP-9500). Interestingly, this satisfying collection includes a live version of "Cocaine" from *The Fool Circle* rather than the *Snaz* version.

The descent into the world of programmed, plastic, synth-pop continued with the September release of *The Catch* (VERL 20), the band's first release on Vertigo. Recording in Scotland for the first time since 1973's *Loud 'N' Proud*, this time the work was done at Castle Sound Studios in Pentcaitland, twelve miles southeast of Edinburgh, with John Eden producing.

It's hard to tell exactly what the lads were striving for with their increasing reliance on machine-made music. A guess is that they were attempting their own version of ZZ Top's successful *Eliminator* but didn't have material that was up to the job. When looking back at this period in the band's history, it is often suggested that they were simply trying to fit in with the 1980s pop rock landscape. But that's not all that was happening musically in 1984. Artists of similar vintage were releasing quality new albums without the added concessions to commerciality. Examples include the Scorpions' *Love At First Sting*, Dio's *The Last In Line*, Roger Waters; *The Pros And Cons Of Hitch-Hiking*, and old touring pals Rush's *Grace Under Pressure*. Even their original mentors, Deep Purple, reunited for the return-to-form masterpiece *Perfect Strangers*.

ALBUM OVERVIEW

The Catch opens with "Party Down," a computer-generated reggae effort (if it's one thing reggae should never be, its computer-generated) with layers of techno sequencers, bright keyboard stabs, clacking percussion, and an acoustic guitar strumming valiantly. A ripping guitar solo from Manny Charlton offers a glimpse of humanity, but it's not enough.

Next is a totally unnecessary updating of the Keith Richards-written Rolling Stones song "Ruby Tuesday" from their 1967 *Between The Buttons* album. If you're going to tackle a Stones track, at least dig out a deep cut. The plodding electronic drums are self-defeating, although Dan sounds at least somewhat engaged.

"Last Exit Brooklyn" is an electro-shock new wave rocker with occasional metallic sparks provided by Charlton. Following that is "Moondance," an original(!) that, thankfully, loses the artificial keyboards for Mark Knopfler-ish guitar work during the verses. Considering how castrated most of the album sounds, they sure had balls to give the tune that title. It's not a triumph of songwriting, but at least it's got a sense of life—that's a *sense* of life, not an affirmation of it.

Clumsy title notwithstanding, "Love Of Freedom" is a welcome return to the group's Scottish roots (a vein they should tap into more often). An epic Celtic ballad with a martial beat, the song explodes with a barrage of massive percussion. Unfortunately, this happens just as the song begins to fade out.

With "This Month's Messiah" Dan digs deep into his black bag of tricks to reintroduce the sinister snarl of old while a metronomic drumbeat frames some welcomed thick guitar riffs from Charlton. Then the band states the obvious with "You Don't Believe In Us" (understandable response: Should we?), a techno-boogie exercise in futility in which the return of too many synthesizers and sequencers doesn't help at all. "Sweetheart Tree" is a gritty barroom blues workout that the album could have used more of—much more.

The Catch ends with "Road To Nowhere" (he album reviews itself!), a cover of the tune written by Gerry Goffin and Carole King. This actually has a decent groove to it, and Charlton pulls out an exemplary solo. With a proper production job, this could have been a real gem.

RELEASE AND RECEPTION

Singles released from *The Catch* include "Ruby Tuesday" with B-side "Sweetheart Tree" in the UK (VER 13) and South Africa, a UK-only twelve-inch featuring "Ruby Tuesday," "Sweetheart Tree," "This Month's Messiah," "Do You Think About It" (VERX 13), and "Party Down" with "Do You Think About It" issued in Spain on seven-inch and in Germany on seven-inch and twelve-inch vinyl. While not a top-tier Nazareth song by any means, the non-LP B-side "Do You Think About It" is still better than at least half the tracks that made it to the final product. How this was left off in favour of dreck like "You Don't Believe In Us" remains a mystery.

November 12 brought the band to the long-running German concert television show *Rockpalast*, where a twenty-song set (only two from *The Catch*) was broadcast on TV and radio. Filmed in Bochum, Zeche, the show is a remarkable document of the band performing well during such an odd time for them.

After opening with "Telegram," they unleash a fierce version of "Razamanaz" that has Manny Charlton (wearing the Bilta jersey he's seen sporting on the album sleeve) soloing with such vigor you'd almost swear Zal Cleminson was back in the lineup. They play "Boys In The Band" at a frantic pace with some popping bass from Pete Agnew and a killer guitar solo courtesy of Charlton. The vocals at the end of "Boys In The Band" and the next track, "Beggars Day," are as potent a one-two punch of metal screaming as Dan has ever produced. His loose mood may be based on the amount of drinking he is seen doing during the gig, but it sure doesn't affect his performance negatively. As on the album, "Ruby Tuesday" has a preprogrammed percussion track laying down a rigid beat while Sweet adds additional basic drum effects and McCafferty conducts the crowd to sing along during the chorus. "Cocaine" is done acoustically, as usual, but with the unfortunate extra element of an artificial drum loop.

Another cut from *The Catch*, "This Month's Messiah," benefits from a steady hard drumbeat and Dan's terrific vocals. As is usually the case with Nazareth, the song is improved upon when aired in the live setting. A delicious middle section swings like nobody's business.

"May The Sunshine" is done with a bit of a heavy hand, effectively removing the light touch of the album recording. A strong version of "This Flight Tonight" leads into "Expect No Mercy," with a new guitar intro and thunderous drumming. This is followed by "Hair of the Dog," which, oddly, quotes the riff from the Knack's 1979 hit single "My

Sharona" at one point. Dan seems to be relishing a return to "Bad Bad Boy," which starts with some searing bottleneck slide work.

The show winds up with a trio of covers: ZZ Top's "Tush," the blues standard "Rock Me Baby," and Chuck Berry's 1959 hit "Sweet Little Rock 'n' Roller" (with some fun audience participation). Dan introduces "Rock Me Baby," saying, "Now I want you to understand, we're going to do this song, then we're going to go out to find a nice German pub. You can do what you like, but I'm going to get drunk, okay?"

With many shows from the *Rockpalast* archives being released over the years, there is no reason why this terrific appearance has not come out as a DVD/CD package.

On November 19, the band appeared in Munich, Germany, part of which was broadcast on the TV program *Rock Aus Dem Alabama*. Filmed at the Alabama-Halle, the band run-through ten songs, including three from the new album. "This Month's Messiah" and "Ruby Tuesday" sound similar to the Bochum show eight days previous, while "Party Down," which was not played in Bochum, offers no real surprises. It's a bit heavier than the album version, but it still suffers from an artificial element. "May The Sunshine" benefits from loud backing vocals courtesy of Agnew and Sweet.

A truly comprehensive home video release would include both the Bochum November 12 and Munich November 19 footage in a single package.

In February, the band appeared at the Vina Del Mar International Song Festival in Vina del Mar, Chile, for a set that was broadcast on local television and radio. Coming from the Quinta Vergara Amphitheatre, the broadcast has some dated video effects (e.g., split screens, slow motion moments), and the band perform on an odd, angular stage dressed with neon bars, but the show itself is terrific. Charlton provides heat and enthusiasm, while McCafferty has a surge of energy, bouncing on the stage during the songs. Surprisingly, Darrell even takes an uncharacteristic drum solo during "This Flight Tonight," of all things.

Still promoting the album, May 13 saw Nazareth film their gig at the Camden Palace in London for the *Live From London* TV programme. This footage is a wonderful companion to the two German

TV broadcasts from the previous fall. Although they only perform one track from *The Catch* (an unsurprisingly strong version of "This Month's Messiah"), this is still essential footage. "I Want To Do Everything For You" has a fantastic guitar solo, while McCafferty, as usual, crawls in deep for a vicious vocal on "Beggar's Day." The most interesting track of the show is the finale, a rare cover of "Ain't Got You" by Jimmy Reed (although surely learned from the 1964 version by the Yardbirds). Unfortunately, the song fades out almost as soon as it begins while the credits roll.

On July 2, 1985, a show at Harpo's in Detroit was broadcast over 98.7 WLLZ radio. The show had a few notable moments. Interestingly, Dan actually changes an early lyric in the show opener "Telegram" to "could be Detroit or LA." When introducing "Ruby Tuesday" from the new album, he states dryly, "It's not available in America at the moment." The final encore of ZZ Top's "Tush" has the added kick of Charlton quoting Deep Purple's immortal "Smoke On The Water" riff.

UK music magazine *Metal Hammer* presented a hard rock and metal festival in Germany on September 14, 1985, headlined by Metallica and Venom. Also present were Wishbone Ash, Warlock, Heavy Pettin', and others, including special guests Nazareth. An official VHS home video featured one song by each band (except Metallica) and represented Nazareth with "Dream On." Considering that the festival was designed to be a heavy music show, it's a bit odd that Nazareth is seen performing a ballad, but there is nothing wrong with the version they lay down. A vinyl bootleg called *Songs For The Lady* (BLADE 1AA2) captures Nazareth's full set with a sleeve featuring an unusual black and white illustration of a bee.

It must be noted that of the nine songs on *The Catch*, only three "Party Down," "Ruby Tuesday," and "This Month's Messiah" have ever been performed live by the group.

The band encountered an unfortunate distraction in 1985 as well. Learning that ex-manager Jim White had issued versions of their albums on his Sahara label, Nazareth were forced to bring legal action against him and have the titles pulled from circulation. The albums pirated by White were *Exercises* (SAH 121), *Loud 'n' Proud* (SAH 123),

Hair of the Dog (SAH 124), *Greatest Hits* (SAH 125), *Close Enough For Rock 'n' Roll* (SAH 126), *Malice in Wonderland* (SAH 127), *Expect No Mercy* (SAH 128), *No Mean City* (SAH 129), *Play 'n' the Game* (SAH 131), *Sound Elixir* (SAH 130), *Rampant* (SAH 132), *The Fool Circle* (SAH 133), *Snaz* (SAH 134), *2XS* (SAH 135), and *20 Greatest Hits* (SAH 137). White also released pirated copies of nine different albums by the Sensational Alex Harvey Band (SAH 111 through SAH 119).

In 1985, Nazareth's ex-guitarist, Billy Rankin, released a new album called *Crankin'*. Recorded in Glasgow, the record features guitar contributions from Zal Cleminson and backing vocals from Dan McCafferty and "Uncle" Pete Agnew. (When released on CD, *Crankin'* omitted three of the songs from the original vinyl issue, including a cover of Bachman-Turner Overdrive's 1973 hit "Takin' Care of Business.")

RE-ISSUES, RE-MASTERS, AND RE-RECORDINGS

The May 13 Camden Place show was released on DVD in 2002, unimaginatively titled *Razamanaz*. The audio from the show was used for the "grey market" CD release *Live From London* (BT 33040), which ends inexplicably with the studio recordings of "My White Bicycle" and "Broken Down Angel." The carelessness with which this CD was thrown together is made painfully obvious by the cover photo, which shows the Zal Cleminson lineup on stage. Clearly, this is not the version of the band heard on the recording.

The 1997 Castle CD reissue of *The Catch* adds two bonus tracks: the great non-LP B-side "Do You Think About It" and a fake "previously unreleased edited version" of "Last Exit Brooklyn." Of course, it is previously unreleased, because, previously, it never existed. It's also not edited in any way with an identical running time as the album version.

The 2001 *Back To The Trenches: Live 1972–1984* two-CD set has three tracks recorded in Slough in 1984: "Ruby Tuesday," "Telegram," and "This Month's Messiah." All three are fine renditions, but it's odd that the order of the tracks has been changed. The actual eighteen-song concert opened with "Telegram," "Ruby Tuesday" was fifth, and "This Month's Messiah" was tenth. There's really no gain in putting "Telegram" after "Ruby Tuesday." The date of this show was October 17, 1984, although this information is left off of the *Back to the Trenches* credits. The source of these three songs seems to be a low-fi audience recording.

Eagle Records' 2002 CD features an extended single mix of "Ruby Tuesday," the Castle edit of "Last Exit Brooklyn," and an "alternate version" of "This Month's Messiah," which is also a fake bonus track with no difference from the album cut. The twelve-inch mix of "Ruby Tuesday" has the chorus repeated after the first and second verses instead of played just once, as on the album.

In 2011, Salvo released a two-CD collection gathering *The Catch* along with its follow-up, *Cinema* (1986). Bonus tracks on this set are the B-side "Do You Think About It," the single version of "Party Down" (which fades early), and, of the upmost interest, seven tracks recorded for BBC Radio 1's *Friday Rock Show* on October 14, 1984. This mini-live album features "Beggar's Day," "Cocaine" (after which Dan exclaims "Terrific singing!"), "Party Down" (with the expected sequencers), "This Month's Messiah" (heavy riffing make this one stand out), "This Flight Tonight," "Bad Bad Boy," and a loose tear through "Teenage Nervous Breakdown."

Cinema
1986–88

BACKGROUND

After the sonic disappointment of 1984's *The Catch*, Nazareth took their time before re-entering a recording studio. When they did, it was with the hard lessons learned from the previous album's mistakes. While still employing a 1980s production aesthetic, the band used their time off to bring a stronger selection of material to the sessions, material that would benefit from the tasteful use of technology, not be stifled by it. The new album was recorded primarily at Pearl Sound Studios in Canton, Michigan, with the title track done at Cava Sound Workshops in Glasgow and Castle Sound Studios in Pentcaitland, Scotland.

Released in February 1986, *Cinema* has a smooth studio sheen courtesy of producer Eddie Delana, but it's not shamelessly overblown at the expense of the songs. Does *Cinema* stand up to such past victories as *Loud 'N' Proud* (1973) or *No Mean City* (1979)? Of course not, but it is an improvement over the uncertain *Sound Elixir* (1983) and *The Catch* (1984).

ALBUM OVERVIEW

Full of booming drums, detailed axe-work, and a crystal-clear separation in the mix, *Cinema* sounds like a proper modern overhaul of the Nazareth values. If the album feels a bit hollow at its core, it's because even with the extra effort, the final results sound under-written.

Opening volley, "Cinema" (produced by Manny Charlton) has a large guitar riff matched with oversized drums. Sure, the primary colour synth notes sound dated now, but at least they're making an effort. "Cinema" is also notable for being the only song in rock history to reference the 1983 film *Jaws 3-D*.

On "Juliet," Pete Agnew's bass guitar threads in between shimmering guitar textures. A galloping electro-rhythm gives "Just Another Heartache" momentum even if it doesn't seem to go anywhere noteworthy. "Other Side Of You" is a speedy, little scrapper that, with a warmer production, could have almost passed for a deep cut on AC/DC's *Flick Of The Switch* (1983). On "Hit The Fan," a chunky muscle riff and deep bass guitar form the foundation of this acceptable effort with expressive screeching from McCafferty. "One From The Heart" is an agreeable, if slight, slice of pop confection with ringing guitars during the solo.

"Salty Salty" has prime, scratchy lead vocals and some decent call and response guitar work.

A mid-paced anti-discrimination rant, "White Boy," is capped by Dan arguing his case repeatedly, "You wouldn't do that to a white boy!"

"A Veteran's Song" is a war vet lament that strides proudly with a Celtic melody and an emotionally-charged guitar solo, then ends with appropriately military-styled drums.

RELEASE AND RECEPTION

The only single from the album was the title track backed with a live version of "This Flight Tonight" without any chart success. This release appeared in both seven-inch and twelve-inch formats. The original CD release of *Cinema* included the live bonus tracks "Telegram" and "This Flight Tonight" from *Snaz*.

Longtime fan Nick Kotzer caught the band promoting the album in Seattle, Washington, on April 15, 1987: "One of my friends mentioned that Nazareth would be playing at Parker's Restaurant and Lounge in a month or so. I thought no friggin' way would Nazareth play at a small club like that. These guys are world famous; there must be some mistake.

"I contacted the restaurant to confirm the show, asking if it was really Nazareth and not some cover band. 'All the original members?' I asked. 'Yes!' was the answer.

"I was so excited for the show, almost nervous about it. When the moment arrived, they didn't disappoint. Dan's vocals were so razor-sharp it was unbelievable. They were touring in support of *Cinema*, which, being in the USA, I had never heard of. They played three from the new album 'Cinema,' 'Hit The Fan,' and 'Other Side Of You' plus 'This Month's Messiah,' 'Road Ladies,' 'Miss Misery,' and some of the other usual songs from that era. The entire thing was a real treat to witness, such a hard rocking event!"

On May 7, 1986 the band appeared at Out in the Green, an outdoor festival in Dinkelsbuhl, Bavaria, Germany. Filmed for European TV, the set included the new songs "Cinema," "One From The Heart," and "Other Side Of You." All three were performed with extra energy in the live setting. As for the other *Cinema* tracks, "Juliet," "Just Another Heartache," Salty Salty," and "A Veteran's Song" have never been performed live.

RE-ISSUES, RE-MASTERS, AND RE-RECORDINGS

The 1997 Castle CD includes two previously-unreleased demos of "Just Another Heartache" and "A Veteran's Song." The former is played at a much slower tempo than the album version but is fully finished from a production viewpoint. It's an interesting variant that could have easily made the final album's track listing. The Castle liner notes refer to this track as a "previously unavailable mix," which is incorrect, as it is a completely different recording, not just a different mix. "A Veteran's Song" is a bit stripped down but still has a good balance of acoustic and electric guitars, making it another welcomed bonus track. It's a shame that the Nazareth CD reissues don't have more worthwhile additional material like these two songs.

Eagle Records' 2002 CD includes the two excellent bonus tracks from the Castle CD and adds edited versions of "White Boy" and "Cinema." Of these, "White Boy" simply fades early, while the single edit of "Cinema" shaves off a bit of the intro, starting just before the lyrics begin, to no one's benefit.

In 2011, Salvo reissued *Cinema* as a two-CD set with the previous album, *The Catch*. All bonus tracks on this release pertain to the former album. It is unfortunate that the two extra high-quality tunes on the Castle release were omitted from this edition or at least replaced with tracks of similar value.

A 1988 Beatles tribute album *Norwegian Wood* by RAM Pietsch has Dan singing "Come Together" in a relatively subdued voice until the chorus kicks in. The track has a somewhat odd mix of strings, horns, and industrial percussion.

Into the Ring
1986

BACKGROUND

Dan McCafferty's second solo album, *Into The Ring*, was released in 1986, the same year the band issued *Cinema*, apparently because McCafferty and Pete Agnew had a surplus of quality material. Recorded at Chameleon Studios in Hamburg, Germany, *Into The Ring* was produced to a gleaming finish by Christoph Busse. The cover sleeve sports a blurry photo of American football players in direct opposition to the boxing metaphor of the title track.

ALBUM OVERVIEW

Stylistically, the record is similar to other keyboard-washed and programmed drums-filled albums like *The Catch* and *Cinema*, but it is important to note that the album is actually two different sections of music divided between the respective sides.

Things start off with "Into The Ring," a McCafferty-Agnew composition with percolating keys and synthetic drums but fades quickly during the decent guitar solo. "Backstage Pass" (another Dan and Pete job) is a computer dance track with bright synth stabs and a relaxed lead vocal. Oddly, the tune is sung from the viewpoint of a groupie making herself available to a band's road crew to obtain the titular treasure. It's not hard to see why this gender-swapped track didn't fit within the macho framework of classic Nazareth.

A melancholy ballad with dramatic power chords and forceful drumming, "Starry Eyes" (Busse-McCafferty-Agnew) has Dan explaining to a girlfriend why he has to stay out on the road with the simple statement, "I love you, but I love the rock!"

Written solely by McCafferty, "Sunny Island" is laced with a slightly Caribbean feel, extra percussion, some watery guitar, and ends with a breezy saxophone solo. One wonders why they didn't go for more of a soca-reggae feel by using actual steel drums instead of vibes. The song has a protagonist who regrets moving from a tropical location to the literally and figuratively cold New York City.

"For A Car" (McCafferty-Agnew) is a rigid, machine-made slab of keyboard-heavy pop with processed backing vocals from Agnew, who also plays bass on side one of the record.

Written by McCafferty and Agnew, "Caledonia" is a serene epic with Dan more invested in it than anything else on the record so far. Thankfully, the song doesn't have many of the programmed elements found on other tracks. There are some keyboard sound effects, but the entire piece would have been much more effective with traditional Celtic instrumentation.

Side two of the album requires a bit of backstory.

In 1985, German singer-songwriter Hans Hartz released the album *Neuland Suite* (also produced by Christoph Busse), which went to number fifty-seven on the charts in that country. Side two of the record, also titled "Neuland Suite," weaves an epic tale of a group of one hundred dislocated men traveling to find a new life in an unknown country for their families. The track "Sally-Mary" features lead vocals from McCafferty, who is also featured, along with Hartz, in the music video for the song. Music videos were shot for *Neuland Suite*, mostly consisting of generic footage of sailboats and ocean waves, although marching soldiers and a burning grand piano are seen in the "Albatross" clip.

For McCafferty's second solo album, it was decided to re-record the entire second side of Hartz's *Neuland Suite* project, now renamed *Suite: Nowhere Land*, or at least to re-record the lead vocals, as almost all of the music seems to be identical to that heard on the original *Neuland Suite*.

The tale begins with "Headin' for South America" (original title "Wir Fahren Nach Sudamerika"), which has a thumping drum machine, liquid lead guitar, and gang vocals that peter out with a piano and synth fade. In it, we learn that the sailing group are seeking an island and are determined to travel for as long as it takes to find it.

A brief instrumental interlude, "The Departure" ("Die Abfahrt") makes itself known with big, booming drums and a synthesizer playing the prominent lead line "Southern Cross" ("Kreuz Des Sudens") is a laid-back ballad with a vibrant guitar solo and, intriguingly, a dry lead vocal from McCafferty, which is noticeably different from his usual weapon of choice. The weary vocals fit the sentiment of the exhausted traveler who is writing a letter home to a loved one perfectly ("We're still full of hope, although the trip is grinding").

In the style of a vintage rock 'n' roll number, "Where The Ocean Ends" (Hinterm Ozean Liegt Ein Neves Land") has the travelers celebrating their freedom and looking forward to the new life that is surely soon to come. Unfortunately, the track is derailed by the intrusive synthesizer, although it does end with some plaintive horn playing.

The sea chanty "Sally Mary" changes the mood a bit with the flavour of a barroom sing-along. Again, the travelers regale each other with tales of home and the loved ones they left behind. Hans Hartz contributes vocals along with McCafferty, although for some reason he is not credited.

As the title indicates, "Island In The Sun" ("Insel Vor Dem Wind") represents the first look at the end of the group's pilgrimage as a series of islands appear on the horizon. "Island In The Sun" is a bouncy, radio-friendly tune with finger snaps that shift gears to finish with an odd-sounding synth solo. This glimmer of hope leads to the anthemic "Albatross," which, despite being held up high by thick bands of keyboard-constructed pillars, is actually a depiction of bleak disappointment at finding the coveted promised land already barren at the hands of man.

The album ends with "We've Been A Hundred Men" ("Die Letzen Mussen Die Ersten Sein"), which reveals that out of the original one hundred people who started this trip, only ten have survived. This is a piano ballad with a sensitive McCafferty vocal and an explosive middle section before settling down. The track includes a brief instrumental reprise of "Headin' For South America" to indicate the broken group turning around and starting the long, depressing journey home before ending with a rare bit of spoken dialogue from the singer.

Strangely, although the entire saga is one that it would seem to take place many decades ago, where yearlong journeys by sea could be imagined, *Suite: Nowhere Land* (and its original German rendition) actually occurs from August 15, 1989 to September 1990.

RELEASE AND RECEPTION

A single of "Starry Eyes" with "Sunny Island" on the B-side (888 397-7) was released in Portugal in 1987 in a picture sleeve but without any chart action.

The initial CD of *Into The Ring* (830 934-2) was released in Germany by Phonogram in 1987. Although the titles on the back cover are the same English ones mentioned above, inside the accompanying lyric booklet are a couple of interesting differences. Track ten is called "Where The Ocean Ends We'll Find a New-Born Land," and the fourteenth cut, "We've Been A Hundred Men," is called "The Last Ones Will Be The First After All," which is actually the correct translation of the original German title, "Die Letzen Mussen Die Ersten Sein."

Renaming the song "We've Been A Hundred Men" was a curious and unnecessary decision.

RE-ISSUES, RE-MASTERS, AND RE-RECORDINGS

When Nazareth albums first surfaced on counterfeit Russian CDs in 1998, *Into The Ring* was paired with *Single Hits vol. 3*

In 2002, Eagle Records in Germany issued *Into The Ring* on CD as a two-disc package with Dan's 1975 self-titled solo album. This set includes two bonus tracks, single edits of "Sunny Island" and "Starry Eyes," which are mislabeled on the back artwork as each other. The bonus track "Starry Eyes" omits fours lines of lyrics in the middle of the song and fades a bit early to reduce the track by about a full minute. The so-called "single edit" of "Sunny Island" actually runs about twenty seconds longer than the album version.

Salvo declined to make the Dan McCafferty solo albums part of their Nazareth CD reissue series, but then in September of 2013, they released *Into The Ring* digitally through iTunes. This digital download does not include the single edits of "Sunny Island" or "Starry Eyes."

Snakes 'n' Ladders
1989

BACKGROUND

After a gap of over three years, in January 1989, a new Nazareth product was released. Recorded at Comforts Place Studio in Lingfield, Surrey, England, and produced by Joey Balin, *Snakes 'n' Ladders* was released on Vertigo Records in Europe and Japan. The album was not available in North America or the UK

ALBUM OVERVIEW

The album opens with "We Are Animals" (renamed "Animals" on subsequent CD releases), which has a stiff, clanging rhythm and a preening lead vocal. The relative highlight is songwriter Manny Charlton's slide guitar solo.

"Lady Luck" is a smoldering blues track with sturdy performances from all involved. Luckily, it's produced with an appropriately warm feel that the album needs way more of. A cover of Tim Hardin's 1966 song "Hang On To A Dream" (originally titled "How Can We Hang On To A Dream" on his *Tim Hardin 1* album) has rigid percussion, a yearning vocal, washes of synthesizer, and some bright, if infrequent, splashes of guitar.

Next up is another cover, "Piece Of My Heart," done originally by the underappreciated Erma Franklin in 1967 but more well known by the 1968 cover by Big Brother and the Holding Company, featuring Janis Joplin on their classic *Cheap Thrills* album. What must have looked good on paper, Dan's drinking man vocals replacing Joplin's whiskey-soaked yearnings, is rendered pointless by the lukewarm arrangement and questionable "borrowing" of Whitesnake's "Here I Go Again" guitar riff. And let's not pretend that the Whitesnake appropriation is some sort of nod to the album's title. That's a bit too clever for this lot.

On "Trouble," we have hard, calculated production barely salvaged by Dan's snarling vocals. As usual, he does most of the heavy lifting.

Another Charlton composition, "The Key" is a modern funk exercise with a typically tasty slide guitar solo from Charlton, but not much else is worth noting. "Back To School" has a patient, keyboard-spattered groove that inches its way forward before thick power chords take over during the chorus for some much-needed additional authority. "Girls" is an okay rocker that speeds along fine if one ignores the sub-Nikki Sixx lyrics ("Some girls do it, some girls won't").

Regarding Charlton's next composition, "Donna—Get Off That Crack," what's the point of an anti-drug song if it's on an album no one is ever going to hear? Or if they do, it may make them want to be under the influence.

"See You, See Me" has McCafferty wailing over ringing guitar textures and also features a serviceable axe solo and a pleasant, jangling tambourine. The guitar solo is unlike anything heard in Charlton's history. The album limps over the finish line with a bland cover of Neil Young's "Helpless" from the Crosby, Still, Nash and Young's *déjà vu*

(1970). This version has the added distraction of programmed percussion, plastic keyboards, and the sound of waves crashing on a beach.

RELEASE AND RECEPTION

"Piece Of My Heart" was released as a single in Germany with "Lady Luck" on the B-side. A twelve-inch vinyl single and a CD single added "See You, See Me" to the package.

Shortly after the *Snakes 'n' Ladders* sessions, the McCafferty composition "Winner of the Night" was produced by Charlton, to be used as the theme music for a German TV program. Unfortunately it's another generic, mid-tempo pop number with a supposedly uplifting lyrical message if one isn't too depressed with the state of affairs with this once-mighty band. The song was released as a single in Germany and the Netherlands with the *Snakes 'n' Ladders* track "Trouble" on the B-side. A twelve-inch vinyl single and a CD single add smoking live versions of "Woke Up This Morning" and "Bad Bad Boy" recorded in Illertissen, Germany on July 22, 1989 which are essential listening.

This version of "Woke Up This Morning" begins with searing slide guitar before the impressively large drums kick in. This cut has driving vocals and an extremely large sound, as if it was recorded in an arena and not the smaller venues the band was relegated to frequenting at that stage in their career. The track ends with a wonderful flurry of slide guitar notes. Dan's tough vocal on "Bad Bad Boy" and the terrific performance from the band make it clear that, despite what was happening on the studio albums, the guys were still hitting the stage with power and authority. Maybe a sequel to *Snaz* should have been considered.

Years after the original album's release, Pete Agnew revealed that, at the producer's insistence, the majority of the guitar, bass, and drums were recorded by session musicians. This explains the guitar sound heard on "See You See Me." If correct (and going by the sound of the album and the album credits, it seems to be), *Snakes 'N' Ladders* is less an underperforming Nazareth release than an unofficial third Dan

McCafferty solo album, albeit one with the vocalist seemingly in a hostage situation without his bandmates.

To promote the album, the band hit Germany for a hearty eighteen dates in October with Canadian rocker Lee Aaron opening. A circulating tape from one of the German shows has Nazareth performing a heavy version of "Razamanaz" and "I Want To Do Everything For You" with an extra bluesy ending that leads right into the *Snakes 'n' Ladders* cut "Lady Luck." They also do "Piece Of My Heart" and "Hang On To A Dream," and "Cocaine" gets a humorous dedication to their record label. "Cocaine" has an extra bass guitar and percussion breakdown that is a pleasant surprise. "Hit The Fan" from *Cinema* has better-than-usual drumming, but the talk box fails Dan on "Hair of the Dog."

A truly historic show occurred on May 13, 1990, at East End Park in the boys' hometown of Dunfermline, Scotland. A benefit concert to raise funds to buy sports wheelchairs that was, fortunately, broadcast on the radio, this concert also featured ex-Marillion vocalist Fish opening the show.

Taking the stage, appropriately, to the sound of pipes and drums, Nazareth tears into an excellent rendition of "Telegram" before delivering "Razamanaz" with loud backing vocals courtesy of Pete Agnew. Next, the band plays the bluesy beginning of "I Want To Do Everything For You" as the intro to the *Snakes 'n' Ladders* track "Lady Luck." Dan's vocals get an extra layer of echo for "Piece Of My Heart" before the highlight of the gig is unleashed.

"Morning Dew" begins with marching drums and gets an incredible, extended guitar solo from Manny. It's a revelation to hear the track restored to its former glory after the odd 1981 rerecording. In fact, this version is better than the song has ever sounded.

To follow that memorable performance, the band *really* breaks out the big guns. With opening act Fish on lead vocals (Dan provides high backing vocals), Nazareth rips through an adrenalized cover of "The Faith Healer." Originally recorded by the Sensational Alex Harvey Band on their 1973 album *Next*, this stands as the only time Nazareth ever played the song. It's a rare moment in Nazareth history and gives the entire gig a special status.

Unfortunately, as noteworthy as the concert is from a set list point of view, it's also historic for a less than celebratory reason. This hometown gig was Manny Charlton's last with the original group he helped rise to stardom in the 1970s. (The *Back to the Trenches* CD liner notes state that he left the band on May 7. If true, perhaps the benefit show was something he had already agreed to do.)

RE-ISSUES, RE-MASTERS, AND RE-RECORDINGS

In Italy, issue eighty-two of music magazine *Il Rock* included a free compilation, which split sides by Nazareth and their old touring partners, Kiss. The Nazareth tracks are "Boys In The Band," "All Nite Radio," "We Are The People," "Love Leads To Madness," "Razamanaz," and "This Flight Tonight." The cover sleeve to this untitled LP depicts live concert shots of both Dan and Gene Simmons (circa 1975). The Kiss songs on the second side are "I Love It Loud," "Love Gun," "Shout It Out Loud," "Detroit Rock City," "I Was Made For Loving You," and "Rock 'N' Roll All Nite." Also released in 1990 was the album *Tongue 'n' Groove* (recorded in 1989) by singer-songwriter Michael Patrick with Dan contributing backing vocals to "When It's Over." It's a decent, mid-tempo, pop-rock tune, although McCafferty is far back in the mix.

The 1997 Castle CD (the album's first release in the UK) adds three bonus tracks. First is "Winner Of The Night," which is from the same era, so it belongs with this release. Next are the two commendable live numbers from the "Winner Of The Night" twelve-inch single: "Woke Up This Morning" and "Bad Bad Boy."

Eagle Records' 2002 CD reissue has the bonus tracks "Hang On To A Dream" (single edit), "Lady Luck" (extended version), "We Are Animals" (alternate edit), and "Trouble" (single version). These are all fake. "Hang On To A Dream" and "Trouble" were never issued as singles, so crediting them as such is offensive.

Much more interesting is a batch of rare *Snakes 'n' Ladders* outtakes that were released on the *The Naz Box* four-CD boxed set (2010). A strong and hearty reading of Cream's "Sunshine Of Your Love" (from 1967's *Disraeli Gears*) is balanced by an uncharacteristically restrained lead vocal from McCafferty. Compared to the thick riffs being piled on, he croons the song, and the juxtaposition is refreshing. If they had to have a cover tune on the finished album, this should have replaced one of the songs that made the final track listing. "Heatwave" is a pleasantly noisy, if questionable, take on the 1963 hit by Martha and the Vandellas, and we are finally treated to the demo recording of the album track "See You, See Me." The extra aggression and explosive guitar solo make this cut a worthwhile alternate to the album take.

Salvo's 2011 two-CD set combines *Snakes 'n' Ladders* with the follow-up record *No Jive* and includes the same three bonus tracks that appeared on the 1997 Castle release.

No Jive
1991

BACKGROUND

Nazareth's next album represented an unthinkable lineup change for the long-running institution. Original guitarist Manny Charlton had left the band. Reports at the time stated that Charlton had been fired, although since then, the split has been attributed simply to "creative differences." In fact, the *Naz Box* liner notes state that he quit. For his replacement, Nazareth called back former member Billy Rankin to step into the frontline position.

Before entering a recording studio, the newly re-vamped group hit the road to play some gigs that had already bene booked in the US with Ten Years After and Blackfoot plus some European dates with Kansas, Styx, Uriah Heep, and Wishbone Ash. Then, on December 12, 1990 the new Billy Rankin-led Nazareth performed a momentous concert in Rio de Janeiro.

Opening With "Night Woman," the band wastes no time stating their intention to impress. Following with an a capella cover of a song by the legendary Lefty Frizzell is one of the shows many highlights. Frizzell's 1959 recording of "Long Black Veil" hit number six on the charts and has been covered by artists like Johnny Cash, Joan Baez, and the Band among others. McCafferty's rendition, with harmonies courtesy of Pete Agnew and Billy Rankin, is pure perfection.

After a smashing version of "Big Boy," Dan introduces "Right Between The Eyes," saying, "We're gonna do a song now you've never heard before. This is brand new! It was written by Billy," previewing a track that appeared on the next album. Other highlights of the 1990 Rio show are the buzzing guitars on "Love Hurts" and Rankin's interesting solo during "Hair of the Dog," which touches on Manny Charlton's version but adds aspects of the new guy's personality as well.

On February 9, 1991, the band played a determined set in Tallin, Estonia beginning with extra guitar sparks from Rankin on "Night Woman." He also tried out some new parts during "Bad Bad Boy." A programed beat threatened to drag "Cocaine," although Sweet added some percussive embellishments for a bit of humanity. A new cut "Right Between The Eyes" had an energetic run-through, the band clearly enjoying testing fresh material in front of an appreciative crowd. An awkward attempt at "Animals," however, didn't seem worth the effort. The show ends with "Tush," featuring an extended and noisy solo from Rankin.

A show at the Music Halle in Frankfurt was filmed for German television, giving fans a good look at the new lineup. At the end of "Razamanaz," Rankin's lead guitar playing is so incendiary that he breaks a string, necessitating a quick change of weapon (swapping a Gibson Les Paul for a Gibson hollow body).

After "I Want To Do Everything For You," Dan introduces the band, and then the show takes an odd turn. A traditional Scottish pipes and drums group comes out on stage along with a young woman wearing a giant cake costume. McCafferty jokingly introduces the pipers as his sons and then, referring to the woman, states, "And this is my wife!" Then he clarifies, saying, "Actually, what it is, this is a birthday cake, 'cause we've been doing this for twenty years now," and then he recoils in mock horror.

Another moment of levity occurs later in the show when Dan introduces "Whisky Drinkin' Woman" by saying, "It's a song about my mother."

After some time at Shorties Rehearsal Studios in Dunfermline to get material together, the band took over production responsibilities at CAS Studio in St. Ingbert-Schurev, Germany, in a bid to restore their former glory. From a pure musical standpoint, they came pretty close.

ALBUM OVERVIEW

The record begins with the notable increase in heft that is "Hire And Fire," featuring razor-sharp guitars, larger than usual drums, and unfortunate Def Leppard-sounding back-up vocals. The track also begins with a noticeable resemblance to Black Sabbath's "Supertzar."

"Do You Wanna Play House" has a stuttering riff and pounding drums, while Rankin's solo takes aim at the stratosphere briefly before getting distracted by closer targets. The tune also has the appearance of *Hysteria*-sounding back-up vocals, an effect that, thankfully, doesn't appear again on the album. A caffeinated little mover, "Right Between

The Eyes," is by Billy Rankin, who also contributes some screaming axe work. The fourth cut, "Every Time It Rains," is a big, commercial power ballad, proving that the band has not quite kicked some of the previous five years' bad habits.

"Keeping Our Love Alive" is an anonymous, mid-tempo, slightly dance-style tune with handclaps and a Mark Knopfler-ish guitar solo. An upbeat, driving, four-on-the-floor rocker, "Thinkin' Man's Nightmare" has McCafferty singing the verses in a lower range before returning to his trademark rasp come chorus time.

"Cover Your Heart" is a poppy Rankin number with a sticky chorus and multiple guitar tracks crashing into each other. If the band and/or label were serious about pursuing chart success, why was this not released as a single?

A throbbing grinder with real meat on its bones, unfortunately, "Lap Of Luxury" is plagued by processed backing vocals that reduce the song's sonic strength.

The next piece is a medley. "The Rowan Tree" is a traditional Scottish ballad performed instrumentally by Rankin's clean acoustic guitar. This leads directly into marching drums, which signal the switch to "Tell Me That You Love Me," a Celtic-sounding track with mandolin high in the mix and some crushing guitar riffs.

The album finishes off with "Cry Wolf," an acceptable, rowdy rocker—well, 1991's version of a rowdy rocker anyway.

As a bonus track, at their new record company's insistence, the band re-recorded their 1973 song "This Flight Tonight," with predictable results. There is absolutely nothing wrong with the re-recording, just that the exercise seems pointless, since it's unlikely such a thing can compete with the prototype. There's also a difference between the youthful innocence of the original performance and a completely unthreatening retread eighteen years later.

RELEASE AND RECEPTION

No Jive was released in Europe on the Mausoleum label in November of 1991, hitting number thirty-one in Austria and number thirty-six in Switzerland.

The first single from the album was the Belgium release "Every Time It Rains," paired with "This Flight Tonight 1991." It was followed in Germany by a CD single and a twelve-inch single consisting of "Every Time It Rains," "This Flight Tonight 1991," and "Lap Of Luxury." A European CD single contained "Tell Me That You Love Me," "Right Between The Eyes," and "The Rowan Tree—Tell Me That You Love Me."

Unsurprisingly, the single version of "Tell Me That You Love Me" removes the "Rowan Tree" acoustic intro to shorten the track.

A promo CD sampler issued in the US consisted of "Do You Wanna Play House," "Right Between The Eyes," and "Hire And Fire." A limited edition of just one thousand copies of the album on CD packaged in a leather sleeve and featuring the bonus track "This Flight Tonight 1991" was available in the US. A music video for "Tell Me That You Love Me" shows the band miming on a massive stage while models cavort in the background.

On June 13, 1992, the group performed a noteworthy show at the Lycabettus Theatre in Athens, Greece. The concert was plagued by technical problems, which the band complained about openly. As they tend to do when equipment issues come up, the guys broke out a mostly a cappella version of "Long Black Veil" to buy time for the sound crew to fix the problems.

Three songs from *No Jive* were played well ("Hire And Fire," "Do You Wanna Play House," and "Right Between The Eyes"), and the group's old touring partner, Deep Purple front man Ian Gillan, joined for an informal run-through of "Tush" and "Smoke On The Water." What the performance lacks in finesse it makes up for in exuberance, and hearing the two leather-lunged vocalists combining their firepower is noteworthy, if only for the rarity of the occasion. Gillan was touring

Europe to promote his latest solo album *Tool Box*. By August he rejoined Deep Purple on a full-time basis.

What does a hardworking band do to relax before they start the next leg of a tour? Why, start up another band, of course.

The Party Boys was a loose collective of Scottish musicians, including Dan McCafferty, Zal Cleminson, Chris Glen, Ted McKenna, Ronnie Leahy, and others.

From late 1992 into the first few months of 1993, the Party Boys played a series of small gigs around Scotland.

A show on December 17 at the Music Box in Edinburgh was broadcast on local radio, revealing an engaging mix of tunes. New song "Tell Me That You Love Me" from the *No Jive* album got a healthy reading, while Billy Rankin took lead vocal chores for a laid-back "Rocky Mountain Way" and ex-Marillion vocalist Fish handled the Sensational Alex Harvey Band selections "The Faith Healer" (*Next* 1973) and "Boston Tea Party" (*SAHB Stories* 1976) as well as a cover of Argent's 1972 hit "Hold Your Head Up" from the *All Together Now* album. For "You Got Me Humming," from Dan's solo album, Dan was joined by Nazareth comrade Pete Agnew for the duet parts. After that, Dan sang the SAHB tune "Midnight Moses" (from the 1972 album *Framed*). The broadcast ends with a great take on ZZ Top's "Tush," where Pete Agnew actually gets some lead vocal opportunities. The highlight of the show has to be the surprising choice of Prince's "Electric Chair," a deep cut from the 1989 *Batman* soundtrack.

The set list for a show at Glasgow venue Rocking Horse included Frankie Goes To Hollywood's "Warriors Of The Wasteland," three songs from the *Dan McCafferty* album ("Whatcha Gonna Do About It," "Stay With Me Baby," and "You Got Me Hummin'"), and a cover of Jerry Reed's "Amos Moses," as recorded on SAHB's 1976 album *SAHB Stories*.

On January 31, 1993, the group played a great set at the White House in Hill O'Beath near Dunfermline, consisting of a killer version of "Electric Chair," ZZ Top's "La Grange," "Stay With Me Baby," "You Got Me Hummin'," "Tush," and the SAHB fave "The Faith Healer," with lead vocals from McCafferty, who, unsurprisingly, makes the song his own.

Other songs played at various gigs include David Bowie's "Ziggy Stardust," the 1973 Ike and Tina hit "Nutbush City Limits," Frank Zappa's "Road Ladies," and "Armed & Ready" by The Michael Schenker Group (ex-SAHB members Ted McKenna and Chris Glen were also in the early 1980s lineup of Schenker's band). They also played a fantastic version of Mr. Mister's 1985 hit "Broken Wings," with expressive McCafferty lead vocals and some terrific guitar playing.

In 1993, the Party Boys evolved into a SAHB reunion, which resulted in the concert document *Live In Glasgow '93*.

A visit to Bob's Garage on KZOK radio in Seattle bore a raw recording of "Hair of the Dog," which Dan introduced as "a song about my father." Rankin adds a few bold bits of flash to the tried and tested muscle riff.

Nick Kotzer was at the July 22, 1993 concert in Eugene, Oregon: "This was an awesome concert surrounded by a bunch of rowdy college-aged kids out for a good time. Did Billy Rankin ever kick ass! They were supporting *No Jive* and opened with 'Hire And Fire.' They also played 'Vigilante Man' and 'Gone Dead Train,' if you can believe that, plus a few songs from *No Jive*, of course, including 'Play House.' When 'Right Between The Eyes' came up, the crowd in front was head banging their heads off. It was a beautiful sight.

"Nazareth was back, as far as I was concerned, and I was so happy for the band. I loved Manny's work on the albums, but it doesn't get any better than Billy playing live. He just had a feel for the crowd, the original intent of the songs, and put his own style and energy into one incredible performance. In my opinion, Billy Rankin fit perfectly with the band live and in the studio. Shame it didn't last."

Richard Kolke witnessed the November 6, 1993 show at the Commodore Ballroom in Vancouver: "Setlists.com says there was a show on November 5 as well, but I'm pretty sure there wasn't. There were four bands on the bill, and Nazareth was headlining. The other acts (in order of appearance) were Wishbone Ash, Uriah Heep, and Blue Oyster Cult.

"I am not that familiar with Wishbone Ash, but I was pretty impressed with their performance, even they only got about thirty minutes. They were a tight band and rocked hard, a great opening act.

"Uriah Heep was next, and although I was a big fan back in the David Byron days, I was unimpressed with their show. Mick Box was the only band member I recognized, and after opening with a couple of tunes, I recognized they played mostly newer songs, which I didn't know and didn't care for. On the rare instance that they played a tune I recognized, it was pretty terrible, probably because lesser musicians were trying to duplicate the Byron and Ken Hensley's performances. They played for about forty-five minutes, but it seemed a lot longer. A few people in the crowd seemed to really like the set, but I wasn't one of them.

"On the other hand, Blue Oyster Cult delivered a cracking performance. In the hour they were allotted, they played most of their best-known tunes and even delivered a first-rate performance of "Astronomy," one of my favorite BOC numbers. They closed with '(Don't Fear) The Reaper' (of course) and had the crowd on their feet for the first time that night.

"Finally, Nazareth came on. I hadn't seen them live since 1975, when their opening act was Rush. I knew Manny wasn't in the band anymore, but I hadn't heard any of their recent material.

"They opened with 'Telegram,' and I knew immediately that something wasn't right. Dan McCafferty was having big problems hitting any of the high notes, and Billy Rankin's guitar had a thin, reedy sound to it. I had thought they might just need to get warmed up, but, unfortunately, it didn't get any better. I know he's not Freddie Mercury, but Dan seemed to be having big problems with his voice—he might have been really sick, for all I know. Also, the absence of Manny Charlton's guitar really affected the arrangements. Rankin was unable to play a power chord to save his life and instead just played flashy leads over everything, which didn't suit the music at all. Especially after the professional show staged by BOC, it was quite a letdown. A lot of people seemed to enjoy it, but Nazareth didn't get nearly the ovation that BOC did."

Here is the set list, as best as Richard can recall:

Set list

1 — "Telegram"
2 — "Razamanaz"
3 — "I Want to Do Everything for You"
4 — "Alcatraz"
5 — "My White Bicycle"
6 — "Whiskey Drinkin' Woman"
7 — "Bad Bad Boy"
8 — "Vigilante Man" (Richard notes this one was especially painful—both the singing and guitar playing.)
9 — "Hair of the Dog"
10 — "Love Hurts"
11 — "This Flight Tonight"

Encores

1 — "Broken Down Angel"
2 — "Tush"

Jon Hahn caught the tour a couple of weeks later on November 27 in Valley Forge, PA: "The show was a multi-group tour thing. I forget what it was called, something like Dinosaurs of Rock. It featured Wishbone Ash, Uriah Heep, Nazareth, and Blue Oyster Cult all in the same concert! It was an event tied in with what used to be an awesome record show that holiday weekend held at a hotel/convention center that was near the concert venue. This was back before the Internet, Amazon, etc., so that was the place to go to buy all the rare, latest, and even bootleg music you could get your hands on. The record show was tied into a sponsorship with a local radio station, as was the concert.

"Members from all of the bands attended the record show on Saturday as celebrity guests available to meet, get autographs from, etc. I used to have a tour T-shirt of the show that I had autographed by all the band members who were at the meet and greet, but I think I actually sold it on eBay a couple years ago, if you can believe that!

"The concert was at a place called the Valley Forge Music Fair, which, sadly, is no longer with us. It was a unique venue with a circular, rotating stage that was positioned below the level of the audience, except for the first two rows or so. I was in the first row.

"If I recall correctly, the order of the acts was Wishbone Ash, Uriah Heep, Nazareth, and then BOC. Wishbone Ash only had about thirty minutes. I think Heep had about forty-five, Naz had about an hour, and BOC between sixty to seventy-five minutes.

"One of Wishbone Ash's signature songs is 'Blowing Free' from their *Argus* album. It features a distinctive opening riff/chord shape based on an open D-chord up the neck, kind of similar to the Who's 'Underture.'

"When Nazareth took the stage, about an hour or so after Ash was done, before Naz started playing, while they were just getting ready checking their sound levels, Billy Rankin played the 'Blowing Free' riff, just joking around, and he even laughed about it! Probably not many people noticed, but I got a kick out of that.

A friend of mine taped the show on a dinky cassette recorder. I think I used to have a copy, but I no longer do."

RE-ISSUES, RE-MASTERS, AND RE-RECORDINGS

Also out in 1991 was an odd-looking compilation, simply titled *Nazareth* (MHRL-1087), that was produced in South Korea by Mun-Hwa Records. The sleeve sports a stylized painting of a bird flying through a lighting storm while the album itself is comprised of "Love Hurts," "Sunshine," "Razamanaz," "Shanghai'd In Shanghai," "Bad Bad Boy," "Woke Up This Morning," "Hair of the Dog," "Holy Roller," "This

Flight Tonight," "Broken Down Angel," "Expect No Mercy," "Turn On Your Receiver," and "My White Bicycle."

The 2002 Eagle Records *No Jive* CD has the bonus tracks "Hire And Fire" (edit version), which just fades early, as most fake bonus tracks do, and "The Rowan Tree—Tell Me That You Love Me" (extended version), which is absolute nonsense. First, the acoustic guitar introduction has actually been edited out (unbelievable on a so-called "extended version"), which means that "The Rowan Tree" portion of the medley is absent despite the track's title. Second, near the end of the song, an entire section is repeated to lengthen the track artificially.

The 1993 album *Going Home* (EDL 2736-2) by German group Seasons features Dan singing the title track, a romantic lament that, thematically, would have fit perfectly on his 1986 *Into The Ring* solo album. Speaking of which, *Going Home* includes an excellent re-recording of the track "Caledonia" from that release. The new version even improves upon the original with a warmer sound and more organic instrumentation. McCafferty is also one of four vocalists (along with Ian Cussick, Drue Williams, and Susanna Reed) trading verses on the spiritual standard "Amazing Grace." An outtake from *Going Home*, "No Turning Back" is a decent, mid-paced tune with a catchy chorus and relatively clean McCafferty vocals. Two singles were released for this project, each with one of the songs on which Dan appears. "Slowly The Snow's Falling" paired with "Amazing Grace (EDL 2769-5) and "Going Home" with "Journey To Scotland" on the B-side (EDL 2749-5).

Released in 1993 was a four-track CD single of "Morning Dew," as remixed by someone going by the handle "Orange." The different tracks include a "rock version," a "radio version," a "trance mix," and a brief instrumental called the "nuclear fallout version." All of these retain elements of the band's original recording augmented with thumping dance music dressing. The intended market for this travesty remains unknown.

In August 2015, Billy Rankin offered free downloads of demo recordings from the *No Jive* sessions. Of these, an instrumental version of "Hire And Fire" slams with energy, and it's a treat hearing early versions of "Wanna Play House," "Right Behind The Eyes," "Keeping Our Love

Alive," "Cover Your Heart," "Lap Of Luxury" (with some slippery bass playing), "Tell Me That You Love Me," and "Cry Wolf." Also included are two takes of "Every Time It Rains," both of which are missing the guitar solo, although they do leave a few bars where it appears on the finished track.

Move Me
1994

BACKGROUND

Touring through the summer of 1994, a June 3 festival show at Stoenerock Wiesen Prados in Austria saw none other than Lemmy Kilmister from Motorhead join the band to play Pete's bass during "Hair of the Dog" and "Tush" (not "Expect No Mercy," as some claim). Lemmy also contributed backing vocals in his trademark growl on "Hair of the Dog."

The sonic retooling of Nazareth continued with Billy Rankin standing his ground, taking on more songwriting responsibilities and ensuring that new material was, first and foremost, six strings-driven. Of the eleven tracks on the new album, an impressive eight are credited solely to Rankin, who also received co-writing credits on the remaining three songs.

Returning to CAS Studios in Shuren, Germany, Nazareth teamed up with Tony Taverner to handle the production. Taverner was no stranger to the group, having engineered their 1975 album *Hair of the Dog*.

ALBUM OVERVIEW

Loud guitars and slamming drums introduce "Let Me Be Your Dog," and McCafferty sounds completely engaged and rejuvenated, clearly enjoying the new band flexing it's muscles.

On "Can't Shake Those Shakes," a thick, funky guitar lick permeates the gritty landscape while extra percussion is provided, appropriately, by handheld shakers.

"Crack Me Up" has a snarling guitar riff that twists itself through the electric romp while staying out of the way of McCafferty's entertaining performance.

The ballad "Move Me" features acoustic guitars, some subtle percussion, and a subdued lead vocal. Best of all, Rankin's electric guitar playing is determined, and no synthesizers are present.

Not only is "Steamroller" a great thudding rocker with an unrelenting guitar figure throughout, lyrically, it actually mentions Scottish pop group the Bay City Rollers!

"Stand by Your Beds" is mid-paced, but Dan reverts back to his mid-1970s roar during the line "By your beds!"

"Rip It Up" is a chugging, little scrapper saddled, unfortunately, with anonymous backing vocals.

A barroom sing-along, "Demon Alcohol" has a fluid guitar solo over a bed of acoustic strumming and ends with a bit of a cappella vocals from the lads.

"You Had It Comin'" is a basic but satisfying rock tune, the verses of which resemble the Gene Simmons-written Wendy O. Williams 1984 track "It's My Life."

Copious drums start the sporty "Bring It On Home To Mama" to great effect, or perhaps it's just a relief to hear real flesh and blood drumming on a Nazareth record again.

The album winds up with "Burning Down," which, while taken at a slower tempo, isn't really sentimental enough to be considered a ballad. And there's nothing wrong with that.

RELEASE AND RECEPTION

Upon release of the album, a CD single was issued in Germany consisting of "Move Me," "Steamroller," "Let Me Be Your Dog," and "Rip It Up" (853 713-2).

The album itself reached number thirty-six on the charts in Switzerland. A US promo CD sampler consisted of "Move Me," "Love Hurts" (orchestra version), "Razamanaz" (acoustic), "My White Bicycle" (acoustic), and "This Flight Tonight" (acoustic).

The acoustic version of "Razamanaz" sounds quite different until the lyrics kick in. It is strummed pleasantly and has handclaps to further bolster the track's uplifting vibe. It is an inoffensive exercise to all but the coldest of hearts.

The arrangement of "My White Bicycle" doesn't stray too far from the band's original take, but it does have great vocal accompaniment from the group.

Of the three acoustic tunes, Joni Mitchell's "This Flight Tonight" gets the most radical reworking, with a springy rhythm, before the chorus reverts back to the album arrangement. Rankin adds a Delta blues-style slide guitar solo that is sublime in its tastefulness. An acoustic album of originals should have been considered at that point.

With time to kill before rehearsals for the *Move Me* tour began, an acoustic tour was arranged during November 1994 with less than a dozen gigs in Scotland. The shows were held in small clubs and pubs featuring Dan, Pete, and Billy, as there was no need for drums.

On November 30, the trio played in Cumbernauld, where "Razamanaz" was looser than ever, and a really interesting "Big

Boy" was presented. Other highlights were the unexpected "Simple Solution," "Hair of the Dog," introduced as a song "made famous by Guns N' Roses," some excellent vocal harmonies during "Long Black Veil," and a gorgeous "Broken Down Angel" that repeatedly quotes the guitar parts from Rod Stewart's "Maggie May." For "This Flight Tonight." Rankin dispenses with his usual guitar solo and plays the one from the song "Roll Over Lay Down" by Status Quo (from their 1973 album *Hello*).

Michael Tasker reports from Scotland: "I attended the Edinburgh gig, and it was a very informal affair with the guys telling jokes and stories between songs. All very relaxed and fun. The standard of musicianship was superb, and it was a treat to hear Dan and Pete singing harmonies on so many songs."

These were Billy's last gigs before he was dismissed from the band in December 1994. With his unfortunate departure, the majority of the *Move Me* material lost its chance to be performed live. In fact, only two songs, the title cut and "Steamroller," have ever been played in concert.

RE-ISSUES, RE-MASTERS, AND RE-RECORDINGS

In 1994, the band re-recorded their 1974 song "Love Hurts" with the Munich Philharmonic Orchestra for the TV mini-series *Scarlet* starring Joanne Whalley and Timothy Dalton. The orchestra adds an extra layer of dramatic effect, but when Rankin struggles to be heard during his solo, things have gone too far. This new version of "Love Hurts" reached number eighty-nine on the German charts.

Eagle Records' 2002 CD boasts a selection of bonus tracks without any value at all. The extended version of "Let Me Be Your Dog" merely repeats the first verse near the end of the song to pad out the running time while edited versions of "Can't Shake These Shakes" and "Move Me" simply fade slightly earlier than the album takes. The "Love Hurts" instrumental orchestra version is pointless.

In August 2015, Rankin offered free downloads of ten demo recordings from the *Move Me* sessions for fans to enjoy. "Let Me Be Your Dog," "Move Me," and "Bring It On Home To Mama" have perfectly acceptable lead vocals from the guitarist while "Crack Me Up," "Steamroller," "Stand By Your Beds," and "Demon Alcohol" feature McCafferty's early take on the material.

Rankin's rendition of "Move Me" is notable for the sparse electric guitar on the track, which was replaced by an acoustic for the album take.

Two takes of "Steamroller" offer slightly different lyrics than the album version, and, in fact, both early demos do not yet have the Bay City Rollers mention heard on the final cut. An instrumental run-through of "Steamroller" has intense, in-your-face drumming and loud guitars, making it one of many highlights of the demo tape.

The a cappella harmonies at the end of "Demon Alcohol" are even better on the demo than on the final album.

Boogaloo
1998–2001

BACKGROUND

For the band's twentieth studio album, they met with producer Mike Ging at Parkgate Studio in Catsfield, East Sussex, England, and went to work. It was spring 1997, and the album took over a year to complete due to interference from the band's record company, who insisted on changes to the mix. At a show in Seattle on July 30, 1997, Dan stated, "We just finished a new album. It's called *N*." In Vancouver on October 25 of the same year, he introduced the new song "Open Up Woman" by saying, "We have a new album coming out next year, and it's called *N*."

Nick Kotzer attended that show: "I would call this an educated Nazareth crowd; they knew most of the songs. You know how some folks play air guitar or sing along during shows? Well, I was an air drummer right up front next to the stage. I could see Darrell was watching me, too. They played 'Big Boy,' 'Heart's Grown Cold,' 'Java Blues,' and more plus 'God Save the South' from the upcoming album. At the end of the show, Darrel crossed the stage and handed me his sticks. It confirmed that he was watching me! After the show, he gave me a drum lid and signed my sticks."

In early 1998, the band continued working on the album to fulfill the record execs' wishes, adding more guitar to the mix and a horn section comprised of Simon Clarke (Deacon Blue, Suede) on alto and baritone sax, Tim Sanders (David Gilmour, Rolling Stones) on tenor sax, Paul Spong (Wet Wet Wet, Rolling Stones) on trumpet, and Roddy Lorimer (the Waterboys) on trumpet.

During the delay of its release, the album title was changed from *N* to *Boogaloo*. One song from the original *N* album was left off the final release. All others were given additional polish, as was the directive from the group's label.

ALBUM OVERVIEW

The album enters into consciousness with "Light Comes Down," a low-slung bit of menace that benefits from a warm organ sound and Dan's devilish lead vocals.

"Cheerleader" is a busy, little blur of a track with pronounced piano from Leahy and lead vocals that switch channels a few times. Next up is "Loverman," where organ stabs and bright horns bring to mind the funky strut of prime 1970s Aerosmith (Dan even cops a Steven Tyler lick at one point). Unfortunately, it also has the smooth studio sheen of freeze-dried 1990s Aerosmith.

"Open Up Woman" boasts waves of gritty axe work, a sizzling solo from Murrison, and a wailing lead vocal.

Composed by keyboardist Ronnie Leahy, "Talk Talk" opens with a sequencer pattern before, at Darrell Sweet's insistence, the guitar enters to add some needed heft. This track also has a hint of the old glam rock stomp.

The beginning of "Nothing So Good" has some atmospheric guitar (including backwards effects) before kicking into a full-on raver. As usual, the star of the show is Dan McCafferty's expressive sandpaper vocals.

"Party In The Kremlin" starts with funky sequencers, where a Hammond B-3 would have done the job. Lyrically, this one would have fit in just fine on *The Catch*.

"God Save The South" is a decent barroom blues workout, with the horn section adding the necessary accompaniment.

Dan takes a deep breath and lets loose a nearly non-stop, rapid-fire vocal on "Robber and the Roadie" while the piano riffs along with a gruff guitar.

"Waiting" follows, a hard, mid-paced, to-the-point groove with additional percussion contributed by Pete's son Lee Agnew.

The final track "May Heaven Keep You," begins in the usual ballad territory before dramatic power chords take flight. It's still a pretty standard ballad, but at least there's an element of drama to it. The song was released originally as a lush single sixteen years earlier (in 1982) by children from Crossford Primary School in Fife, Scotland. Written by Pete Agnew and featuring accompaniment from Agnew and Billy Rankin, this rarity was produced by Manny Charlton. The re-recording on *Boogaloo* states that the writing was a joint effort between all 1998-era members, a generous gesture on Agnew's part.

RELEASE AND RECEPTION

Boogaloo was released in August 1998. On August 25, the band made an appearance at the Phoenix Club in Toronto. Although the venue could hold 1,350 people, only a few hundred supporters came out. If the lads were concerned, they didn't let on. Throughout the show, Pete Agnew grinned like he'd just won the lottery, and Dan gave an arena-worthy performance. Backstage after the show, the group was not bothered in the least by the low turnout, chatting happily with friends and fans.

Of the eleven songs on the album, only five have never been performed live "Cheerleader," "Loverman," "Party In The Kremlin," "Robber And The Roadie," and "May Heaven Help You."

In April 1999, the band began the second leg of the US *Boogaloo* tour. A show on April 24 at The Kake Boone Country Club in Raleigh, NC featured rock solid renditions of four new tracks "Lights Come Down," "God Save The South," Talk Talk," and "Nothing So Good." A pleasant surprise was the return of Rick Danko's chunky "Java Blues" to the set list, although Murrison's lengthy guitar intro to "Whiskey Drinkin' Woman" veered suspiciously close to Edward Van Halen's "Eruption," and the synth-laced "Beggar's Day" was unfortunate.

Worse things were waiting in the wings when Darrell Sweet passed away suddenly from a heart attack in New Albany, Indiana on April 30, 1999. After a period of mourning, the band decided to continue with Lee Agnew filling in for Sweet.

During this same period, ex-Nazareth guitarist Billy Rankin released a decent new solo album, *Shake* (1999), a balanced mix of upbeat pop tunes and some harder-edged material. The album boasts bright production values, razor-sharp guitar playing, and Rankin's excellent lead vocals. "Walk Out" is an enjoyable exercise in modern funk, while "Get Inside You" strides forth with large, imposing riffs. Artistically, the album was another successful release for the talented singer-songwriter.

RE-ISSUES, RE-MASTERS, AND RE-RECORDINGS

When touring commenced, fans who had been hungry for live product had their answered. A series of limited edition "official" bootlegs became available through the band's website. Among the shows released (unfortunately on cheap CD-RS, not pressed CDS) were Aschaffenburg Germany (January 28, 2000), Kitchener, Ontario (July 22, 2000), Leamington, Ontario (July 23, 2000), Barrie Ontario (July 28, 2000), Port Dover, Ontario (July 29, 2000), Ionia, Michigan (July 31, 2000), Rochester, Michigan (August 1, 2000), Columbus, Ohio (August 10, 2000), Pardubice, Czech Republic (November 15, 2000), Pilsen, Czech Republic (November 17, 2000), Pilsen, Czech Republic (November 18, 2000), Salzburg, Austria (January 25, 2001),

Baar, Switzerland (January 27, 2001), Hamburg, Germany (January 29, 2001), Denver, Colorado (2001), Rice Lake, Wisconsin (2001), Wheeling, Wyoming (2001), and Palatka, Florida (May 25, 2001).

For our purposes, we'll be looking at the July 22, 2000 recording (NAZ BOOT 3) from the Lyric Theatre in Kitchener, Ontario. Two songs from *Boogaloo* were performed: a strong "Lights Come Down" and "God Save The South" done with more of a bluesy edge than on the album. "Holiday" has some new, odd-sounding keyboards, but the guitar riffs are thick and satisfying. "Miss Misery" from 1975's *Hair of the Dog* is delivered with simmering, street-level intensity and then downshifts into even darker territory with a portion of "Please Don't Judas Me" (also *from Hair of the Dog*). The merging of these two tracks is so successful one wonders why they weren't always been played this way.

A bit of a surprise in the set is "Sunshine" from 1974's *Rampant*. A less enjoyable aspect is the dated, plastic keyboards that open the vintage track "My White Bicycle."

An interesting moment occurs during Dan's introduction of "Beggar's Day" when he states, "Okay, this is the CanCon section. We're gonna do one now that was written by a Canadian chappie, a man called Nils Lofgren wrote this. We recorded it." It provides much food for thought. First of all, it is impressive that McCafferty is aware of the CanCon ruling, a controversial Canadian broadcasting requirement to ensure a certain amount of homegrown talent is given quality airtime. Second, it's a bit odd that McCafferty thinks this song meets CanCon regulations, as Lofgren is actually a born and bred American artist.

For "Hair of the Dog," Canadian drummer Barry Connor (Toronto, Coney Hatch, Lee Aaron) is introduced to contribute the cowbell part, while "Cocaine" is given a terrific electric arrangement.

Darrel Sweet's legacy was celebrated through the hard work of fan Brian Baxter, with contributions from fellow supporters. On May 8, 2001, a smartly designed memorial plaque to the deceased drummer was installed at the New Albany Riverfront Amphitheatre, the unfortunate place of his untimely passing.

In 2001, AC/DC vocalist Brian Johnson embarked on a brief UK reunion tour with his earlier band Geordie. A highlight was a fun run-through of the Nazareth arrangement of "This Flight Tonight" with Johnson remarking "by that Dan McCafferty fella." For fans who have long thought the two vocalists had a similar sound (the song "Hair of the Dog" being exhibit A), hearing Johnson tackle the tune brought the comparison full circle.

In 2011, Salvo reissued *Boogaloo* as a two-CD set with the previous album *Move Me*. This package included two bonus tracks "Laid To Wasted" and "Walk By Yourself." Both tracks were on the 2001 release *The Very Best Of Nazareth*, while "Walk By Yourself" also appeared on *Maximum XS: The Essential Nazareth* in 2004.

"Laid To Wasted" is a haunting piano ballad with yearning lead vocals and an economic guitar solo. An earlier attempt at the song occurred during the 1983 sessions for the *Sound Elixir* album, that outtake ending up on 2001's *The Naz Box* collection. The second version changes the instrumentation somewhat with the addition of Ronnie Leahy's piano "Walk By Yourself" is a solid, tightly-wound piece of work with a funky start-stop groove and warm organ playing throughout and is completely album-worthy.

In 1998, a proliferation of counterfeit Nazareth CD sets were produced in Russia, combining two albums into a single two-CD package with questionable sound quality. Among the pirate releases are *Nazareth/Close Enough For Rock 'n' Roll* (CDM 193-44), *Razamanaz/No Jive* (CDM 198-46), *Rampant/Play 'n' the Game* (CDM 198-48), *Expect No Mercy/The Catch* (CDM 198-49), *No Mean City/Cinema* (CDM 198-50), *Malice In Wonderland/The Fool Circle* (CDM 198-51), *Snakes 'n' Ladders/Single Hits vol. 1* (CDM 698-129), *Move Me/Single Hits vol. 2* (CDM 698-130) and *Into The Ring/Single Hits Vol. 3* (CDM 698-131). Even shoddier Russian releases include *Exercises/Hair of the Dog, Loud 'n' Proud/2XS, Play 'n' The Game/Close Enough For Rock 'n' Roll* and *Sound Elixir/Dan McCafferty*.

Homecoming
2002–2007

BACKGROUND

Some twenty years after the landmark live album *Snaz*, Nazareth descended on the Glasgow music venue the Garage to record the long awaited follow up. Less a concert than a gathering of the faithful, the November 20, 2001 show was a celebration for the fans as well as the musicians onstage. Some of those devotees traveled the globe to witness the festivities. The official document of this event, *Homecoming*, was released in April 2002 in both CD and DVD formats, since the concert was filmed as well. Both versions have the same song lists, although the CD has some stage banter edited out, and the DVD contains bonus interview footage.

As for those supporters who trekked to big show, Ian Naismyth did just that: "I flew to Scotland from Vancouver for the event with my buddy Ed. We arrived in Dunfermline at around five in the evening, totally jetlagged from our long flight on the Friday afternoon.

"After we'd dropped our bags at my sister's house, where we were staying, we headed for a splendid dinner party at the Pitbauchlie Hotel, which Ronnie Dalrymple (a Naz lighting tech at the time) and his lovely wife Bev had organized. In fact, they organized the entire weekend for everyone, and they did a marvelous job, too. It was great to walk into that room and find around forty-five to fifty members of the international Naz Army. I had met some previously, and others were merely names on the Internet forum. After dinner, copious amounts of alcohol were consumed, but since Ed and I had been awake for thirty hours or so, we called it quits much earlier than some.

"The next day, I took Ed on a tour around my hometown, and everywhere we turned, more Naz shirts were around the corner like it was an invasion.

"That evening up in that famous pub called Sinky's, we all amassed for another evening of revelry with the promise from our hosts, Ronnie and Bev, of a 'surprise guest.' After several more drinks, who should arrive but Billy Rankin. He entertained us for the entire night, and I believe most people filmed it.

"The next afternoon, we all met at Sinky's once again. After a few hours of partying, were poured onto buses, which took us over to Glasgow and the venue known as the Garage.

"Naz put on a fantastic show, as evidenced in the video. The only unexpected event was a small fire in the balcony where the video crew were. Apparently, someone had left an extension cord looped on the floor, which gave it the effect of a heating coil, and it burst into flames. It was not a major fire, but when doused with an extinguisher, the overspray fell onto some of the crowd toward the back and made for some difficult breathing. Some people simply moved forward a bit whilst others took an adjacent staircase down and came right back up on the other side of the room. I don't think the band even knew what happened, and they didn't miss a beat."

Russ Evers was also there: "Many fans of the band from various countries attended the gig, and several met at a few venues near to the venue prior to the show. I traveled up from Wolverhampton in England (about a six hundred-mile round trip) to be there, having first seen Nazareth in Wolverhampton in February 1979 on the *No Mean City* tour.

"The atmosphere at the venue was great. It was sold out, and I would estimate a crowd approaching one thousand. I was at the front, and at one point notified Tam Sinclair that Jimmy's amp was belching smoke and in danger of catching fire!

"That problem aside, Naz, Dan in particular, were in fine form, and the crowd response was phenomenal. It was both a surprise and a disappointment that the crowd reaction did not come across very well on the CD or the DVD. The only other thing was that the keyboards were very low in the mix and filled the empty spaces well, but on the CD/DVD, the keyboards are much higher and clearer and seem to detract from the power of Jimmy's playing. All in all, it was a great night."

Helge Rognstad also attended: "I was there, and it was a great night. Lots of fans from all around Europe and even Canada. It was like an international convention centre in the lobby before entering with all the different languages being spoken.

"One of my best memories was Dan popping out after the gig to invite everyone to the local pub for a pint. Needless to say, Sinky's was crammed to the rafters that night. I have lots of stories but none suitable for print. Another great memory was meeting Darrell's family. It was very emotional for a lot of people, as it was just a couple of years after Darrell's passing at that point."

The surprise Billy Rankin performance to which Ian Naismyth refers consisted of the ex-Nazareth guitar slinger playing a twelve-string, entertaining the faithful with fantastic versions of favourites like "May The Sunshine," "Love Leads To Madness," and "Heart's Grown Cold" plus relative rarities like "Every Time It Rains," "Games," "All Nite Radio," and "Demon Alcohol." He also offered an odd cover of Britney Spears' "Baby One More Time" to the music of Led Zeppelin's "Stairway to Heaven," to the delight of those attending.

ALBUM OVERVIEW

The band begins with "When the Lights Come Down," the opening track from their most recent studio album, *Boogaloo*, with a deep, powerful groove and excellent lead vocals. Guitarist Jimmy Murrison also explores some expansive frequencies during his solo. The classic guitar riff to "Razamanaz" is doubled by Ronnie Leahy's keyboards, softening the attack somewhat.

The medley of two tracks from 1975's *Hair of the Dog* album, "Miss Misery" and "Please Don't Judas Me" is near perfection. The secretive "Simple Solution" from 1978's *No Mean City* adds a bit more drama to the otherwise jubilant proceedings and has Leahy alternating between electric piano and a warmer organ sound. However, on "My White Bicycle," treacly keys fight for space during Murrison's guitar solo.

A new track, "Walk By Yourself," recorded specifically for the 2001 compilation *The Very Best Of Nazareth*, is a tough, to-the-point rocker with decent riffs and a typically raw McCafferty vocal.

Unfortunately, the extended piano intro to "Heart's Grown Cold" cannot compete with the definitive Manny Charlton-Zal Cleminson guitar opening statement from 1980's *Malice In Wonderland* tour. Luckily, once the song gets going, Murrison and the younger Agnew bring some needed authority.

"Broken Down Angel," from *Razamanaz* (1973), features some fervent crowd singing during the chorus, to be expected with some of the most devout Naz maniacs in the audience. For "Whisky Drinkin' Woman," Leahy plays horn parts on his keyboards, an odd choice, since there wasn't a horn section on the original recording. McCafferty brings his A-game for "This Flight Tonight," but, unfortunately, some stiff piano pounding occurs during the lines "they're singin' goodbye, baby, baby, bye-bye" and "hope they've finally fixed your automobile" that is just awkward and distracting. The show ends elegantly with a sparse reading of "Love Hurts."

RELEASE AND RECEPTION

Homecoming was rereleased in 2003 as a budget-priced CD titled *Alive & Kicking*, omitting seven tracks ("Holiday," "Dream On," "Simple Solution," "Walk By Yourself," "Heart's Grown Cold," "Hair of the Dog," and "This Flight Tonight"). It was reissued again in 2013 in the UK and Europe (reverting back to the original *Homecoming* title) as a two-disc set combining both the CD and the DVD editions.

The DVD edition of *Homecoming* includes interviews with the individual band members (Dan and Pete together), although the editing seems a bit rushed. Often, the last word of an answer is faded out before the end of the sentence. At one point during Jimmy Murrison's segment, the interviewer says, "Many people consider this to be the definitive lineup," which, considering that this version of Nazareth had yet to record a single studio album seems like quite a stretch. During Lee Agnew's interview, he announces that "As long as you've got Dan McCafferty singing, you'll have that Nazareth sound."

On September 2, 2002, Nazareth participated in an all-star benefit concert for respected Scottish singer-songwriter Frankie Miller, who had suffered a brain hemorrhage in 1994 resulting in a five-month coma. Taking place at the Barrowland Ballroom in Glasgow and broadcast on FM radio, the show had Nazareth performing Miller's song "Danger Danger" before being joined by Big Country's Bruce Watson for additional guitar power on a blend of "Hair of the Dog" and "Broken Down Angel." Among the others performing at the gig were Brian Robertson (Thin Lizzy, Motorhead) and SAHB, consisting of ex-Nazareth guitarist Zal Cleminson, Hugh McKenna (keyboards) and Ted McKenna (drums), all three of whom played on the 1975 *Dan McCafferty* solo album. This SAHB lineup also included original bassist Chris Glen. Filling in for the departed Alex Harvey was another ex-Nazareth axe slinger, Billy Rankin. A highlight of their set was a brooding version of "Faith Healer" with rowdy vocals from Rankin.

On December 19, 2003 Nazareth headlined a special charity show held at the Glen Pavilion in Pittencreif Park in Dunfermline. With all proceeds going to MacMillan Cancer Relief, the show, produced by

Ronnie Dalrymple and Bev Harrison, featured local acts Lights Out By Nine and Satellite Falls (which included Lee, Stevie, and Chris Agnew) plus the then-newly formed duo of Bruce Watson (Big Country) and J.J. Gilmour (the Silencers). There was also a charity auction where, among donations from AC/DC, Deep Purple, Bon Jovi, and the Average White Band, was Dan's striking red and white Marlboro leather jacket seen in so many promo photos around that time.

Lensed at Shepperton Film Studios in Shepperton, Surrey, England in July 2005, *Live from Classic T Stage* is a bit different from the usual rock concert DVD. Yes, the band does rock out on a nineteen-song selection of recent cuts, classic hits, and deep tracks. And yes, both the sound and the picture quality are as dynamic and crystal clear as anyone could hope for. In fact, you've rarely seen the frontline so exposed under mostly hot white lighting. Jimmy Murrison's gold Gibson positively glows on screen.

What sets this release apart from most concert DVDs is the unusual aspect that there is no audience. Nazareth submits a perfectly enjoyable performance to an empty television studio. If there is a lack of focus due to the crowd-less format, it sure isn't noticeable, but it does seem a shame that no one aside from a few cameramen were present to witness such an intimate showing.

The gig itself includes a smoldering "Kentucky Fried Blues" and some excellent twelve-string acoustic guitar on "Sunshine." The version of the rarely played "Love Leads To Madness" has strong vocal harmonies and some tougher guitar riffs near the end. For "Heart's Grown Cold," Lee Agnew begins the song up with the frontline with tambourine playing but runs back to his kit when it's time to add some important bashing. A fun moment occurs in "Shanghai'd in Shanghai" when Pete Agnew gets a lead vocal opportunity, singing the bridge by himself, twice no less. Interestingly, "Cocaine" is given a full electric treatment, a bit of a surprise considering the track has always been an acoustic highlight of the live show.

The *Live from Classic T Stage* DVD has two bonus segments as well. "On the Road with Nazareth" is a seventeen-minute piece in which Dan and Pete talk about what touring is like and share a cute Alex

Harvey story. "Nazareth in Germany" is a twenty-four-minute mini-documentary from the band's 2005 tour. This portion shows the band rehearsing, playing, and conducting interviews on the road (the sound quality during the interviews is very poor).

On September 23 and 24, 2006, a pair of extraordinary shows in Nazareth's long history were performed as part of a festival commemorating seven hundred years since Robert the Bruce was crowned King of Scotland. The setting for these historic, sold-out concerts was the Carnegie Hall in Dunfermline, a venue the band had not played since 1973.

Just before the show began, Dan mischievously peeked his grinning face through the curtain. Once that drape was drawn, a dramatic backdrop was revealed. Two bright shafts of light intersected in front of a large, dark blue background, creating a simple yet effective St. Andrews Cross.

The band members took their places quickly, Agnew at a small drum kit, Murrisson and Agnew Sr. seated with acoustic instruments. Joined by local fiddler Pete Clark and Brian McAlpine on keyboards, Nazareth opened with a reworked rendition of "Bad Bad Boy" that had Clark playing the classic slide guitar lead part on his violin. "The Rowan Tree" was performed as a poignant duet between Murrison and Clark before the band joined in for the expected run-through of "Tell Me That You Love Me." For "Sunshine," Murrison switched to an acoustic twelve-string guitar, with shimmering results.

An excellent reading of "Big Boy" followed while "Local Still" from 1983's *Sound Elixir* was given new life in a pleasant rendition that marked the song's live debut.

Not surprisingly, "Cocaine" sounded fine acoustically, as that's the primary way they have performed it through the years, although the bright violin gave it a bit of new life. As usual, Lefty Frizzel's "Long Black Veil" was performed with fantastic harmonizing from Dan and Pete. The forty-five-minute set ended with "Broken Down Angel" and was given some lively violin contributions from Clark and rowdy singing from the crowd during the chorus.

The electric set began with dependable Nazareth versions of "Miss Misery," "Razamanaz," "Kentucky Fried Blues," and "This Month's Messiah," after which Clark rejoined the group and introduced a new song he had written called "Lament For Danny And Andrew." Along with keyboardist Brian McAlpine, the six-man lineup presented the haunting yet inspiring piece of work.

The band shifted into heavier territory with "My White Bicycle" which had Clark providing searing violin lines.

Clark and McAlpine left the stage for the band to deliver "Holiday" before a lengthy solo guitar intro to "Heart's Grown Cold" led to a cautious reading of the song until they finally kicked into a full-gear rendition.

"Telegram" and "Shanghai'd in Shanghai" were also performed only by Nazareth.

Clark and McAlpine finally rejoined for "Robert the Bruce," a stormy multi-tiered instrumental anthem.

After "Hair of the Dog" and "Whisky Drinkin' Woman," the one hour, fifteen-minute "electric" set ended with a fairly vigorous take on "This Flight Tonight."

The encore began with Clark playing while making his way through the crowd to the stage to begin "Night Woman." Afterwards, an actor dressed as Robert the Bruce gave an impassioned speech before the next selection. Murrison and Clark performed Robbie Burns' "Scots Who Hae," which was the unofficial Scottish national anthem (before "Scotland The Brave" and "Flower of Scotland"), leading perfectly into "Love Hurts." Brian McAlpine rejoined the band for "Love Hurts" and a final bow before the appreciative crowd. The band played the same set both nights.

Helge Rognstad from the Fluffy Jackets remembers: "The unplugged set was the highlight for me, as they played some rare songs from their back catalogue, including 'Local Still,' 'Rowan Tree—Tell Me That You Love Me,' and 'Long Black Veil.' It was also interesting to hear some songs with the fiddle player, such as 'Sunshine' and 'Bad Bad Boy.'

"After the acoustic set, the big amplifiers were brought out, and Nazareth played a full electric set, this time with fiddle player Peter Clark.

"People came from all over the world to see this concert, including fans from Canada, Scandinavia, Germany, Austria, and the Czech Republic, to mention a few."

Michael Tasker was also there: "The anticipation was electric; you could feel it in the air on the Saturday. Fans from all over the world descended on the band's hometown for a historic occasion. Naz playing Dunfermline was big news, and at the legendary Carnegie Hall, no less.

"To add to the spice, there was the anticipated delight of an acoustic set before the Marshalls were set to eleven.

"The lights went down, and a spotlight focused on the curtains where Dan poked his head out, to much cheering. 'Kooeee!' he said with a big grin. The place erupted. Oh, what a night you can have when you're a Naz fan.

"The acoustic set was 'electric.' A highlight was 'Local Still' with 'Long Black Veil' not far behind. Pete Clark lent a different dynamic with the fiddle. It fit in as if written for the songs.

"The smiles and grins on fans' faces at the interval were visible for all to see. We had been part of something special, and the mighty Naz were about to blow us away with a full Monty set of blistering intensity. Jimmy used three Marshall stacks, leaving no one in any doubt that Dunfermline's finest was still loud 'n' proud.

"After the show, it was back to Sinky's bar for a big Naz get together. The band joined in for some well-earned refreshment. It was getting late, very late, in fact, early in the morning, but when with the best band and fans in the world, who watches the clock? Then, on Sunday night, we did it all again, and why not?"

Dougie Ferguson was also present: "I was only at the Saturday night show, and it was great indeed. The acoustic set was the highlight, especially 'Local Still.' The instrumental tracks 'Robert the Bruce' and 'Lament For Danny And Andrew' were very good. There was also a snippet of the old tune 'Scots Who Hae' between 'Night Woman' and 'Love Hurts.' The chap dressed as Robert the Bruce stood outside

Carnegie Hall before the show and then was at the post-concert party at Sinky's pub later. A good night."

Russ Evers: "Yes, I was there, too, a great couple of shows. Think I still have the T-shirt!"

Grant Finlay remembers: "I only made the electric part of the show on the Saturday, because I had just flown in from Spain after being on holiday.

"After the show, most of the travelling fans, road crew, and some of the band headed back to Sinky's pub, which was owned by the band's road manager Tam Sinclair's brothers. This was where the band rehearsed for years. At the after-show event, most fans including me, said that these shows should have been recorded for a DVD. Most of the crew agreed.

"I'm not sure who, but someone along the way managed to get a local camcorder club to come along and film the second show on the Sunday, which I also attended. This footage has never been released officially, and I don't think it was ever intended to be.

"The only other thing I can add is that the design of the official T-shirt of the gig came from a concept and idea that a friend of the band name Graeme Scott and I came up with. A year or so previous to the Carnegie Hall gig, Graeme and I were tasked with creating a Nazareth programme for the Black Friday Nazareth charity shows held in Dunfermline at Christmas time. We both had the cool idea of having Robert the Bruce holding a guitar for the front page of the program. Graeme went out and shot some pictures of statues, and then the guy at the printers superimposed a guitar into his hands. This was used on the programs, and that image with the Bruce connection was used for the official T-shirts for that gig and around the world on many other Naz T-shirts, backstage passes, and so on. So I guess I'm kind of proud when I see that T-shirt at various Naz gigs, knowing I had a small part to play its design."

A specially curated classic rock festival show including Uriah Heep on October 21, 2006 in Knarvik, Norway was broadcast on European television. The ninety-minute Nazareth set included a careening "This Month's Messiah" with gruff vocals from McCafferty, a lengthy, sensitive guitar intro to "Heart's Grown Cold," and a memorably electric version of "Cocaine."

On April 19, 2007 Nazareth performed an incredible concert at Hellooch in Curitiba, Brazil, which was captured on the CD and DVD releases *Live in Brazil*.

A tribal beat introduction makes its way to some pronounced bass playing until boulder-sized guitar riffs fill the air. Dan's lead vocals reveal "Night Woman" from 1973's *Razamanaz*. Next is a solid, if modern, run-through of that album's title track with some extra guitar shredding near the finish.

After respectable (better than that, actually) versions of "I Want To Do Everything For You," "Alcatraz," and "Dream On," they throw the fans a real curve ball. Dan introduces the next number with, "We're going to make a new CD in October, November. September? And this song, it's a Frankie Miller song which may be on it, okay?" Appearing originally on Miller's 1982 album *Standing On The Edge*, "Danger Danger" is an inspired choice of cover material. The band digs deep into the pulsating groove while McCafferty conjures up a vocal on par with anything he's done in the vast Nazareth catalogue. While it didn't end up on the next studio album, "Danger Danger" is an undisputed gem among an already overall excellent show.

After a fun version of "My White Bicycle," Dan mentions that the show is being filmed for a DVD release. A firm reading of "Holiday" guides us to the melodic, hard rock of "Love Leads To Madness," given extra heft with the addition of Murrison's loud, droning guitar. The party-loving crowd gets in on the action too, with some loud participation near the end of the song.

The sorrowful blues of "Loved And Lost" simmers successfully. Some big guitar slashes from Murrison announce the beginning of "Telegram." He also changes some of the parts during the second movement ("So You Want To Be A Rock 'n' Roll Star").

Dan introduces the next pair of songs, saying, "This is a wee Scottish thing. You can join in if ya like. Please do, it's quite great fun." Murrison displays a softer, respectful touch for the traditional Scottish tune "The Rowan Tree" that, as on *No Jive*, takes us directly to "Tell Me That You

Love Me," which, not surprisingly, has a much more carefree feel when performed live. The catchy, sing-along chorus makes this a hit with the excited and possibly slightly intoxicated crowd.

Dan's jagged vocals give "This Flight Tonight" an extra layer of threat, but by the next song, "Hair of the Dog," he's starting to sound strained. "Love Hurts" has some earnest singing from the audience, but Murrison's solo doesn't seem too planned out, and it flutters from idea to disconnected idea. The guitarist redeems himself with the elegantly epic shapes he throws up to begin the stately cover of Bonnie Dobson's "Morning Dew," which is given a fully conceived performance. "Broken Down Angel" signals the end of the show, where the jovial atmosphere of the song is heightened by gleeful singing from the audience.

Lefty Frizzell's "Long Black Veil" from the April 21 show in Sao Bernado do Campo is included as a bonus track on the CD (and plays during the credits of the DVD). Over simple guitar accompaniment, McCafferty and Agnew blend their voices for a profoundly beautiful moment that is one of the many high points of the package. The *Live in Brazil* set is an excellent live, later-era document that deserved a wider release.

A concert in Minsk, Belarus on October 11, 2007, was captured extremely well for Russian TV. The picture and sound quality are sensational, as is the band's performance. It's valuable to get footage of gems like the electric version of "Cocaine," "Love Leads To Madness," "Turn On Your Receiver," among others, in such excellent condition. The set ends with a surprising rendition of "We Are Animals" from 1989's *Snakes 'n' Ladders* album, proving that even at this late stage, the band are still up for dashing expectations.

Also in 2007, McCafferty and Agnew supplied lead and backing vocals (respectfully) on the song "The Dream I Had" by their old producer friend Roger Glover. The song remained unreleased until the 2011 album *If Life Was Easy*, credited to Roger Glover and the Guilty Party.

RE-ISSUES, RE-MASTERS, AND RE-RECORDINGS

Homecoming wasn't the only new live Nazareth title released in 2002. Ex-guitarist Manny Charlton issued a limited edition "official bootleg" of the band's tremendous July 22, 1989 show in Illertissen, Germany on the *Snakes 'n' Ladders* tour. The album, *Raz Em Alive*, presents thirteen songs from the show, including "Woke Up This Morning" and "Bad Bad Boy," which had appeared on the 1997 Castle CD reissue of *Snakes 'n' Ladders*. Highlights include a heavy version of "Razamanaz" and "I Want To Do Everything For You" with an extra bluesy finish that leads right into "Lady Luck." There is a funny dedication of "Cocaine" to the band's record label execs, and the song has an extra bass and percussion breakdown during it as well. "Hit The Fan" from *Cinema* rocks hard with strong drumming, but on "Hair of the Dog," Dan's talk-box is unresponsive. Charlton

decided to omit "This Flight Tonight" and "Love Hurts" from this release, although they were played at the concert.

Another Hair of the Dog: A Tribute to Nazareth was a twelve-song testimonial with curious results. The arrangements are identical to how the original versions sound, although they are given a slightly heavier reading with vocals provided by the likes of Glenn Hughes (Deep Purple), Paul D'Ianno (Iron Maiden), Doogie White (Rainbow), and Nicky Moore (Samson), among others. What is a bit perplexing, however, is that with such a deep catalogue circa 2002, why were songs that Nazareth simply covered considered necessary for the project? Sure, "Love Hurts" and "This Flight Tonight" make sense, since their association with Nazareth is generally identifiable, but "Piece Of My Heart" and "Ruby Tuesday" could have been replaced with prime, original material for which the band is famous. It is also interesting that Paul D'Ianno's take on "Razamanaz" sounds eerily similar to what future Nazareth vocalist Linton Osborne would do with the song in a few years. Apparently, this album found its way into the hands of a certain ex-Nazareth guitar slinger, as Manny Charlton collaborated with Nicky Moore a few years after this CD was released.

Nazareth's excellent studio recording of "Danger Danger" appeared on the 2003 album *Tribute To Frankie Miller*.

The Newz
2008

BACKGROUND

A full ten years after *Boogaloo* (the longest stretch of studio silence in the band's history), Nazareth returned with an album of new material, the first featuring drummer Lee Agnew. Produced by Jann Rouiller at Strong Reaction Music Studio in Switzerland, *The Newz* delivers a varied balance of hard rockers and mid-tempo efforts with a variety of sounds and techniques.

One notable difference is the change in Dan McCafferty's legendary vocals. Finally, after decades of larynx-shredding exhibitions, some wear and tear is evident in a pinched range not heard before.

BACKGROUND

The new platter explodes with a blast of colourful guitar acrobatics for "Goin' Loco" and then turns into a reliable, if basic, rock track, however, it has an unshackled axe solo midway through.

"Day At The Beach" is a spirited, feel-good cut that swings with some rootsy Rolling Stones-style guitars. This is an encouraging example of being accessible without making concessions to commerciality, although they may have gone too far with the overly poppy backing vocals.

Next up is "Liar," with heavy Sabbath riffs underlying this dark track that also has some barely buried spoken word elements during the fade out. "See Me" boasts bright acoustic guitars (think Everly Brothers with 2008 production values) chiming together to create a pleasant, little number that zips along nicely. The sudden stop-start halfway through is pretty startling though.

Introduced with waves of droning axe work, "Enough Love" is a mid-paced tune with relatively clean and clear vocals, proving that it's only when really pushing his growl does McCafferty show strain. "Warning" is made up of thick riffs and a hammering backbeat courtesy of the new guy, Lee Agnew, making his presence known. Next, "Mean Streets," has a purposeful groove that twists it's way around itself while the seductive lead vocal is countered by a higher-pitched bridge.

Another driving, straight-ahead tune, "Road Trip," is completely inoffensive but also pretty inconsequential. Murrison indulges in some nifty twin leads, which are nice to hear, especially in what is no longer a two-guitar band. The decent ballad "Gloria" begins with gentle ringing guitar notes, and then a sudden crash of noisy power chords kicks things up, as does the technical flash of the guitar solo.

"Keep On Travellin'" is an impatient, little thumper that boasts a swaying guitar part near the end that shifts into chiseled riffing. It's also notable for some fluid Charlton-esque slide guitar and Dan's immortal realization, "Bless my soul, I coulda made a living with rock 'n' roll!"

"Loggin' On," has some shimmering guitar textures turning into a steady pop rock track while Dan laments the new, computerized global village, an already dated complaint in 2008.

"The Gathering" is a striding, mid-paced declaration with walls of dirty guitars crunching away. Murrison experiments with some different textures for the verses while Dan sings in a measured and confidently controlled manner.

The album proper ends with "Dying Breed," a quiet, low-key midnight ballad with a far-reaching slide guitar solo and a regretful lead vocal from McCafferty.

A full five minutes of silence after "Dying Breed" has ended, hidden track "The Goblin King" is revealed. An almost black metal exercise (parody?) with multiple lead vocals, dramatic spoken word, and odd sound effects creates an uneasy tapestry of dark and devilish noise. This is one of the most experimental cuts in the entire Nazareth catalogue.

Even before the album was out, the band played an exceptional show in the town of Frome in Somerset, England on February 13. The healthy sixteen-song set included four from the forthcoming album "Keep On Travellin'," "A Day At The Beach" (with extra echo on the vocals), "Enough Love," and "The Gathering." "Whiskey Drinkin' Woman" started with some interesting guitar textures, and the intro to "Morning Dew" referenced the band's early psychedelic influences.

RELEASE AND RECEPTION

When released in March 2008, *The Newz* reached number fifty-one in Sweden, number sixty-eight in Switzerland, and number seventy-five in Austria.

In addition to the regular CD release, there was a deluxe edition subtitled *40th Anniversary Edition Box*. This collectors' piece includes a Nazareth-centric newspaper and a bonus CD.

The extra disc is comprised of serviceable live versions of "Razamanaz," "Love Hurts," and "Hair of the Dog" plus the music video for the album track "See Me," showing the band cavorting in a small club with fans. Although a satisfyingly strong album, seven of the thirteen tracks would not be played live by the band. "Going Loco," "Warning," "Mean Streets," "Road Trip," "Gloria," "Logging On." and "Dying Breed" were all ignored when the band compiled set lists for the upcoming tour.

On May 29, the band returned to Curitiba, the scene of the extraordinary 2007 recording *Live in Brazil*. Dan mentions the previous DVD release, to great cheers. For the 2008 appearance, the show kicks off with "Beggar's Day," "Razamanaz" gets an extended guitar solo from Jimmy Murrison, "Whiskey Drinkin' Woman" has a slow, atmospheric beginning, and "Expect No Mercy" is given a slightly sped-up runthrough. Best of all, a total of four tracks from *The Newz* are presented, all benefiting from the extra enthusiasm that comes with performing in front of an energized audience.

"Keep On Travelin'," "Day At The Beach" (with even more prominent Stones guitars than on the studio version), "Enough Love," and an incredibly elegant version of "The Gathering" are all given healthy workouts during this well-attended concert. The show was filmed, albeit with a single camera, for Brazilian TV.

RE-ISSUES, RE-MASTERS, AND RE-RECORDINGS

In 2009, Dan appeared on the mid-tempo ballad "I Love You" by Russian band Pushking from the album.

On *The Best Volume 1*, McCafferty joined the band to perform the song live, a moment that was captured on video.

That same year, the band's new record company, Salvo, released the two-CD set *The Anthology*, comprised of thirty-eight tracks spanning the albums *Razamanaz* (1973) to *The Newz* (2008). This collection has a decent booklet detailing the band's history with some seven-inch single sleeves pictured.

Big Dogz/The Naz Box
2010–2013

BACKGROUND

After the depressing drought between *Boogaloo* (1998) and *The Newz* (2008), fans did not have to wait another ten years for the next Nazareth album. *Big Dogz* was released in April 2011, and although somewhat below the compositional standards set by *The Newz*, it still protected the relatively new, harder rock aesthetic they had been perfecting since 1994's *Move Me*. Produced by Yann Rouiller (*The Newz*) and guitarist Jimmy Murrison, the new disc was recorded at Sono Records in the Czech Republic.

Prior to recording, on January 19, 2010, Dan McCafferty was a featured vocalist at a Frankfurt concert *Rock Meets Classic*, which presented hard rock singers performing with an orchestra. McCafferty's all-Nazareth set was comprised of "Dream On," "Hair of the Dog," "Holiday," "Love Hurts," "This Flight Tonight," and "Razamanaz." On February 21 of the same year, Dan joined the Deborah Bonham Band at Rothes Halle Glenrothes in Fife, Scotland for a duet of "Stay With Me Baby" from his 1975 self-titled solo album.

ALBUM OVERVIEW

Opening cut "Big Dogz Gonna Howl" is a slow burner with advancing bass guitar from Pete Agnew, who even gets a little solo microphone action during the chorus.

"Claimed" inches forward methodically with a slithering groove and loud backing vocals, courtesy of Agnew.

Next up, a truly unique track, "No Mean Monster," picks up the pace a bit with some nice, loud, rumbling bass. The song takes the original concept of being sung from the point of view of the 1979 *No Mean City* record sleeve character. The twist is that the song doesn't give detailed background information or backstory about the creature. The narrative is that the monster is aware that he was originally just on an LP jacket, stating, "I was right there on the cover, down with the rats and the bones." He goes on to claim "Y'all thought I was nice when I was just merchandise, but I'm free now!" Dan's vocals are predictably evil sounding, giving an appropriate menace to the character known worldwide as "Fred." Why Iron Maiden has never done this with their respective mascot, Eddie, is a mystery. Maybe they have, and I don't know it.

To balance things out, "When Jesus Comes To Save The World Again" is a sparse exploration with soft acoustic guitars and piano. McCafferty offers an uncharacteristically restrained vocal for the majority, upping things a bit near the end for dramatic purposes. It's a remarkable performance fortified with stirring conviction.

"Radio" is a slightly melancholy—although with a warm, uplifting chorus—ode to listening to the airwaves. Supported by some friendly backing vocals, well-placed acoustic guitars, and a brisk electric solo, this one has too much heart to argue with.

A poignant lament about aging, "Time and Tide" is rendered with all the more impact by the participants' acknowledge of their respective advancing years. Murrison adds a tasteful and fittingly unobtrusive guitar solo, while McCafferty's creaking voice matches the weary sentiment perfectly.

Some meaty riffs are introduced during "Lifeboat" but without much in the way of aggression or enthusiasm. There's a pretty interesting ringing effect during the guitar solo though.

"The Toast" is a tipsy, pumped-up retelling of some boisterous partying ("We're all pretty drunk!") with some lead vocals from Pete Agnew. It also has a purposefully rudimentary guitar solo, because we can't expect Murrison to shred when he's "already messed up," and some humorous dialogue from band manager Alan Cottam during the fade letting Dan know that his ride has arrived. It's probably one of the few hard rock songs with the Scots' Gaelic toast "Slainte mhath" ("good health") as the chorus.

A big, swaggering tale, "Watch Your Back" has particularly searing vocals from McCafferty, while the guitars stride proudly with rock-solid authority. There's also an abrupt gear shift for the bridge and a lovely echo-drenched guitar solo.

Paval Bohaty contributes the piano to the pretty ballad "Butterfly," while Dan offers some heartfelt vocals.

The record ends with "Sleeptalker" a tough, little scrapper with jumpy riffs locked in tight with the drums. This standard rock workout opens up for an introspective and interesting back half, featuring clean, exploratory guitar lines and spoken dialogue elements. It's a successful and curious end to the album.

As part of their new Nazareth catalog reissue program, in September 2011, Salvo released *The Naz Box* as a four-CD set with a healthy balance of album tracks and rarities. Discs one and two present an impressive forty tracks spanning the years 1971 to 2011, from *Nazareth* to *Big Dogz*. The fourteen cuts on disc three are from various BBC radio broadcasts from 1972 to 1975.

Disc four has six songs from the November 24, 1977 BBC recording of Nazareth's Golders Green Hippodrome show and nine rarities from the band's career. Of these nine gems, "Paper Sun" (listed as from 1972–73) is a previously-unreleased mid-tempo song with thick guitars and a few fun drum breaks, which is a bit different for Darrell Sweet. Also previously unreleased, "Storm Warning" is a colourful slice of psychedelic-inspired space rock, although it is doubtful it is of the same vintage as "Paper Sun" despite what the credits say. The boxed set also includes a sixty-four-page book with a good history of the band, some vibrant live shots, and pics of dozens of gorgeous international singles picture sleeves.

RELEASE AND RECEPTION

In addition to the regular version, *Big Dogz* was also released as a two-CD package including a bonus live acoustic disc.

Of the bonus material, "Big Boy" has slightly muffled sound. as if recorded at a rehearsal, but the blend of acoustic guitar, piano. and handheld percussion support the strong lead vocals just fine. A relative rarity, "Simple Solution" benefits from an excellent arrangement, while Agnew's bass guitar keeps the momentum going. "My White Bicycle" is presented in a decent version with drummer Lee Agnew playing congas. Sung softer than it has been in years, "Love Hurts" has a good mix of Jimmy Murrison's acoustic guitar picking and Ronnie Leahy's piano. The drums have a bit of a dull thud sound to them though.

The bonus disc ends much too early with "Open Up Woman" from 1998's *Boogaloo*. Dan lets loose with some inspired metallic screams, recalling his peak period as an arena-rattling vocalist. which contrast nicely with the supple acoustic arrangement.

Of the eleven songs on the actual *Big Dogz* album, only "Big Dogz Gonna Howl," "When Jesus Comes To Save The World Again," and "Radio" were performed live by the band (although "Sleeptalker" did get an airing during the upcoming Linton Osborne era).

Richard Kolke caught the *Big Dogz* tour in Melfort, Saskatchewan: "The July 22, 2011 show was at the Melfort Fairgrounds, and it was the headlining show for the annual exhibition and rodeo. Melfort is the town (well, I guess it's technically a city now) where I grew up and where my dad still lives.

"The show was preceded with chuck wagon races, and then the stage was pulled out on a flatbed truck in front of the grandstand. The grandstand was packed, which would probably mean about twelve hundred people or so.

Tickets were $10.00 plus $10.00 to get into the fairgrounds.

"To be honest, I wasn't expecting much, considering the last time I had seen them in 1993 the show was pretty flat.

To my surprise though, they were quite tight and put on an excellent performance, including the *Biz Dogz* songs that I hadn't heard before. Usually when a band of this vintage plays songs off their new album, it's a cue for a bathroom break, but that wasn't the case here.

"Dan mentioned that he had a friend or a relative (can't remember which) living in Melfort as well, which was news to me. I still don't know who it is.

"The crowd was very enthusiastic, and the one hundred-year-old (at least) grandstand was rocking. The concert ended with a fireworks display.

"It was quite a way from headlining in arenas in the 1970s and early 1980s, but they still put on a top-notch show."

Set list

1 — "Silver Dollar Forger"
2 — "Big Dog's Gonna Howl"
3 — "This Month's Messiah"
4 — "Sunshine"
5 — "Turn on Your Receiver"
6 — "See Me"

7 — "Broken Down Angel"
8 — "Radio"
9 — "When Jesus Comes to Save the World Again"
10 — "Love Leads to Madness"
11 — "Whiskey Drinkin' Woman"
12 — "Changin' Times"
13 — "Hair of the Dog"
14 — "Razamanaz"
15 — "Love Hurts"
16 — "This Flight Tonight"

In 2011, Dan reunited with Russian group Pushking to supply lead vocals on the ballad "My Simple Song" for the album *The World As We Know It* (the release also had vocal contributions from Paul Stanley, Alice Cooper, Glenn Hughes, Joe Lynn Turner, Graham Bonnet, and others). He also performed a duet of "Love Hurts" with Jitka Valkova and the Bohemian Symphony Orchestra. A music video for the song was compiled using footage from the recording session.

On January 12, 2012, Dan and Pete joined Dunfermline cover band the Falcons at Sinky's Pub for a fun and loose run-through of "Razamanaz."

Also in 2012, Dan shared vocal duties on the track "Whisky Wonderland," featured on the self-titled album by German metal band Nitrogods. "Whisky Wonderland" has a slamming Bo Diddley beat to which McCafferty adds his distinctive rasp.

Later in the year, the band Austrian ski team coach Mathias Berthold approached the band about contributing the official song for the team. "God of the Mountain" is a suitably speedy clip with a careening solo, while the slamming rhythm section drives the back end. Lyrically, the song touches on the sport ("From the starting gate to the finish line, I'm gonna make this mountain mine"), and the team themselves ("feel the heart of Austria pounding"). The track was released digitally at the end of October with an accompanying music video consisting of footage of the ski team, although, unfortunately, the band does not appear. A CD single of the track was also released.

In February 2013, the FIS Alpine World Ski Championship were held in Schladming, Austria, where, on February 8, Nazareth played an eighteen-song set. The show included "Where Were You" from 1983's *Sound Elixir*, "Radio," from *Big Dogz* (2011), and, of course, a rumbling grind through the new song, "God Of The Mountain."

RE-ISSUES, RE-MASTERS, AND RE-RECORDINGS

During this period, Salvo also released the two-CD set *The Singles*, comprised of thirty-seven tracks spanning the albums *Nazareth* (1971) to *Move Me* (1994). Of the thirty-seven songs, only eighteen were repeated from the 2009 Salvo compilation *The Anthology*.

The booklet for *The Singles* includes track-by-track notation with pics of single sleeves and/or vinyl labels for every song. Although not noted as such, the version of "May The Sunshine" included is the single edit, which is missing the introduction chorus.

Salvo also released a new Nazareth CD compilation, *Hard 'n' Heavy*, in 2013, which is comprised of eighteen tracks spanning the albums *Razamanaz* (1973) to *The Newz* (2008). Compiled by Keith Fitzgerald, freshly-minted weaponry such as "Light Comes Down" and "Road Trip" sit comfortably next to established heavy artillery like "Hair of the Dog" and "Expect No Mercy." The song "Telegram" has it's categorically non-heavy fourth part appropriately edited out.

Perhaps at some point someone should curate a compilation focusing only on the post-Manny Charlton years. For a band that has dozens and dozens of compilations, why not? It could inspire a long-overdue reappraisal of the respective Rankin and Murrison chapters in the Nazareth narrative.

Rock 'n' Roll Telephone
2014

BACKGROUND

In the summer of 2013, things were par for the course in the Nazareth world. A June 25 show at B.B. King's Blues Club & Grill had an inspired set list including an excellent acoustic rendition of "Sunshine," "Radio" from 2011's *Big Dogz*, an electric "Cocaine," and some deep cuts, such as "Shanghai'd in Shanghai," 'Whisky Drinkin' Woman," and "Woke Up This Morning." Jimmy Murrison, sporting a Dio T-shirt, even got the frontline involved in a little choreography before the solo in "Hair of the Dog."

Early July brought the release of *Before Too Long* by Aberdeen hip-hop duo SHY & DRS, featuring Nazareth contributing to the song

"I've Got (Enough Love)" based on "Enough Love" from 2008's *The Newz*. A music video for the song includes footage of the duo performing the track live with Nazareth at a show at the Brook in Southampton. The single "I've Got (Enough Love)" reached number fifty-seven on the charts in Scotland.

Soon though, a series of events unfolded, changing the Nazareth narrative forever. On July 9, while beginning a tour of Western Canada in Cranbrook, BC, Dan McCafferty collapsed onstage during the first song. The gig was cancelled, as was the rest of the tour. Then, on August 24, at the Summerdays Festival in Switzerland, McCafferty ended the performance after three songs, claiming shortness of breath. A few days later, citing Chronis Destructive Pulmonary Disease, Dan announced his retirement from Nazareth.

Pledging to carry on, and with McCafferty's endorsement, the band held fall auditions with Swedish vocalist Emil Gammeltoft and ex-band member Billy Rankin (who turned down the offer to replace Dan). In February 2014, it was announced that Linton Osborne would be taking over lead vocalist duties.

Born in Edinburgh and raised in Rosyth near Dunfermline, Osborne was a curious choice. Sure, he was a local lad, but his professional experience outside of bar bands, was minimal. (He had released a solo album *Pigeonhole* independently).

As a way to introduce the newest member, Nazareth made a questionable move, rerecording five classic songs with Osborne singing. Unfortunately, this effort allowed fans to compare Osborne to the mighty Dan McCafferty, a duel that even the most seasoned vocalist would have trouble walking away from in one piece. Available to listen to for free on the band's official website, the songs sent the Nazareth fan community into disarray.

"Heart's Grown Cold" opens with delicate acoustic guitar playing but then is thrown for a loop by Osborne's highly mannered vocals. On "Love Hurts," the band plays too heavy-handed, erasing any softness present in the original. The lead vocals sound pinched, and Osborne over-emotes to the point of sounding more like a petulant child than conveying a true sense of sadness. "Broken Down Angel" and "Turn

On Your Receiver" don't fair too badly, but in no way can they compare to the original recordings. Things reach rock bottom during "My White Bicycle," with Osborne sounding like a castrated Bon Scott.

On April 10, the band played their first concert with the new lineup at the Ironworks in Inverness, Scotland. The set list offered a pleasant cross-section of tunes from their career: "Telegram," "Holiday," "Razamanaz," "Turn On Your Receiver," "Love Leads To Madness," "Dream On," "Bad Bad Boy," "Shanghai'd in Shanghai," "Miss Misery," "Beggar's Day," "My White Bicycle," "Heart's Grown Cold," "Hair of the Dog," "This Flight Tonight," "Expect No Mercy," "Love Hurts," and "Broken Down Angel." Reaction to the new vocalist, however, was mixed to say the least.

Nevertheless, the band continued on with a tour of Europe. During the May 27 show at Sokolniki in Moscow, even the band sounds lifeless during "Beggar's Day," which they usually sink their teeth into. Jimmy Murrison's solo in "Holiday" also meanders more than usual.

On June 3, 2014 it was time for a new Nazareth album, and this release was pivotal in the band's career, but not for a reason anyone would expect or enjoy. Recorded at the Sub Station in Rosyth,

Scotland, and produced by Yann Rouiller and Michael Brennan, *Rock 'n' Roll Telephone* was the last to feature founding member and vocalist extraordinaire Dan McCafferty.

ALBUM OVERVIEW

The album introduces itself with the hard rock groove of "Boom Bang Bang," a short tune but one that chugs along with purpose. This cut also has an odd keyboard-sounding guitar solo and a bass and drum breakdown that is too brief.

"One Set Of Bones" is a wide rocker with layers of overdriven guitars. Murrison's solo has a harmonica tone to it that is pretty unique.

A highlight of the record, "Back 2B4," is a warmly-written and performed acoustic number that bounces along nicely. Murrison's electric guitar solo adds just the right amount of flair to the otherwise all-acoustic cut. This sweet, little nugget would sound perfect if the band ever does another acoustic tour, as they did back with Billy Rankin in 1994.

Next up, "Winter Sunlight" is a more traditional acoustic ballad with some delicate picking during the solo, but, unfortunately, it cannot compete with the previous tune in terms of pure songwriting quality.

"Rock 'n' Roll Telephone" begins with volleys of careening guitar sparks and then descends to a low and mean rumbling that takes its time pushing forward. It also has some spoken dialogue just before the guitar solo.

The execution is tight on "Punch A Hole In The Sky," a quick, little near-metal sprinter, but it needs a bit more of a surge to take off like it truly should.

In an interesting change of texture, "Long Long Time" has scratching, a hip-hop beat backing track, and an addictive, infectious melody coasting over it. This blend of modern musical elements is surprisingly effective for the so-called classic rock band.

"The Right Time" is a ballad with sparse instrumentation and a slightly country feel to it that, if explored further, would have added a nice extra flavour to the album. Knowing the guys' respect for Lowell George and Gram Parsons, this isn't a stretch. Murrison contributes a nice acoustic slide guitar solo.

A proud declaration of relevance, "Not Today," has McCafferty gruffly staking his claim, "I can still bring the thunder, still got something to say!" Murrison's dirty, forceful guitars add considerable weight to the message.

A Rolling Stones-style guitar riff propels "Speakeasy" across the playing field, while Pete Agnew's prominent bass playing supports the action. It's a decent track, and that Stones tone is golden.

The album winds up with "God Of The Mountain," the great 2012 song written for the Austrian ski team.

RELEASE AND RECEPTION

Rock 'n' Roll Telephone was released generously as a two-CD set with a bonus disc of additional (and quite worthwhile) material.

Monstrous slabs of grinding guitars and pounding drums sends "Just A Ride" into heavy territory (not a bad thing), which offsets the carefree party vibe of "Wanna Feel Good?" nicely (the song itself is an album-worthy track with Agnew's throbbing funk bass playing).

Next up on the second disc are five live songs presented as bonus material. A raunchy rendition of "Big Boy" from Somerset, England, on February 13, 2008, starts things off, followed by a throat-burning "Kentucky Fried Blues" from Milton Keyes in 2006.

Unfortunately, tinny keyboards derail the version of "Sunshine" from Barrie (July 28, 2000), but that is forgotten quickly with the next track, although the guys make the best of an unfortunate situation with shimmery harmony vocals.

To say that the live, earth-shaking recording of "Expect No Mercy," also from Somerset 2008, is a must listen does not do it justice. The barely contained chaos of this tune surpasses expectations of the 2008 lineup's capabilities. The track begins with some ominous riffing, and then screaming lead guitar is unleashed with lethal precision. There's also an extra level of severity to Dan's battle cry of "Expect no mercy!"

After the incredible performance of "Expect No Mercy," "God Save the South" doesn't have much of a chance to compete, but it's still a decent enough take, and it's nice to get a relatively new song among the classics done live. In fact, presenting more of the current material recorded live would only lead to a reevaluation of the newer stuff.

Although presented as a two-CD set, all of the material from both discs could have easily fit onto a single CD. A better value would have been to add the two studio tracks to the end of disc one (where they belong, really) and have the second disc consist of more live material. Better yet, load as much of the 2008 Somerset gig as possible onto disc two. The show has quite a few memorable moments worthy of official documentation (including four songs from *The Newz*, for example).

Rock 'n' Roll Telephone had some decent chart action upon release, hitting number thirty-one in Switzerland, number thirty-five in Austria, number thirty-nine in Germany, and number fifty-eight in Sweden.

Also in 2014, Pete's son Stevie Agnew released the single "The Fall Of Man," a strong country-blues tune with soulful female backing vocals. Dan McCafferty shares lead vocals with the younger Agnew while Pete provides bass guitar work. A rudimentary music video shows the musicians laying down their respective parts over a generic "rootsy" beige background.

Meanwhile, the re-tooled Nazareth continued their European tour. At an August 23 concert in Suceava, Romania, Osborne says, "We have a new album out," referring, of course, to *Rock 'n' Roll Telephone*, a piece of work he had no hand in creating. During that show, Pete Agnew's harmony singing is actually mixed louder than Osborne's lead vocals. While it is doubtful that this was done intentionally, it shows that Agnew is doing his part in keeping the sound as authentic as possible. On the other hand, Osborne's shrieking during the bridge to "One Set Of Bones" can only cause discomfort.

The summer of 2014 brought a tour of Western Canada, making up for the cancelled 2013 jaunt. During this leg, the band played multiple shows in a variety of casinos and small clubs in British Columbia, Alberta, Saskatchewan, and Manitoba.

By August, they were back in Europe, but a special show was announced for November 14 in London, England. Here is the press release for this event:

NAZARETH LIVE AT METROPOLIS STUDIOS. LONDON.
NOVEMBER 14TH 2014
JUST 125 VIP TICKET HOLDERS WILL ATTEND

Filmed for TV and DVD, this unique concert will allow you to see NAZARETH as you never will again—in a studio/club environment reminiscent of legendary clubs like The Marquee. All guests are part of the filmed show, and VIP treatment starts the moment you arrive at Metropolis Studios. Complimentary drinks are provided on arrival, and you will receive a personalized pass/lanyard.

After drinks, you will be ushered into Studio A, where NAZARETH will perform a blistering concert in a tightly-packed club atmosphere. After show will be in Metropolis Main bar with NAZARETH joining the party for a meet and greet and photographs. Our own photographer will be shooting all evening from arrival to end, and these shots are loaded on line for VIP guests to download hi-res images at their discretion from our microsite.

ALL TICKET HOLDERS WILL HAVE THEIR
NAME ON THE CREDITS OF THE DVD.

All tickets are e-tickets and are on a first come, first served basis. Tickets will be exchanged for your personalized, numbered lanyard upon arrival at the studio.

TICKETS PRICED AT £99.00—ON SALE TODAY

Joe Geesin filed this report of the show at www.metaltalk.net:

"Although there had already been some performances with new vocalist Linton Osborne, this was a real fan-oriented launch as well as a show to record a new DVD. With tickets available online and all ticket holders credited in the DVD, this project also saw Nazareth working again with artist Rodney Mathews, who was in attendance on the day with a gallery showing his work (originals, prints, and preliminary sketches), which has adorned posters, calendars, and albums by Magnum, Praying Mantis, and Eloy as well as Nazareth.

"The event kicked off for many at lunchtime, where the film crew interviewed several 'super fans,' some of whom had flown in from around the world, before I was able to interview the band.

"When the doors officially opened at 7:15, fans were able to mix, and I was able to chat with many former Razamanewz subscribers and others I'd met at Darrell Sweet's funeral. Rodney Matthews was there, too, having his photo taken and signing many an autograph.

"The gig itself was in the small room, much wider than deep, barely able to hold the 125 people there, and the heat quickly became unbearable.

"The band seemed happy, taking to the stage, following the intro from Classic Rock's Jerry Ewing. The first few tracks were (not for the only time in the evening) played quickly and consecutively, almost medley-like. I got the feeling this was due to a combination of settling, testing the situation, and nerves.

"They started with 'Silver Dollar Forger,' an old Naz standard, and 'Sleeptalker' (from *Big Dogz*), a solid recent number. The surprise was the third track, "When The Light Comes Down," from *Boogaloo*—an excellent track from an oft-overlooked album.

"Performance thus far—good, slightly muddled, but generally solid, and Linton's voice excellent. His range was good and more often than not suited the songs.

"Now, let's get something straight: Linton is not Dan, and he is not trying to be. Shit happens, and it has happened, and this is proving a launch into a new era. And when Linton settled, you could see the smile broaden, and he started to talk to the crowd, too. The new album's title track followed, then the classic "Razamanaz," a number you all should know.

"Jimmy Murrison played a good riff and a mean solo, and Lee was solid on drums. But for me, the star of the show was bassist Pete. Given what he's been through and what happened last year, it was great to see him playing, and playing so well.

"'Miss Misery' stuttered, a break two minutes in laughed off before the song restarted, but that aside (and the temp-induced detuning in the encore), the set list was excellent, as the two latest albums were represented by a couple of tracks, and then there was pretty broad coverage.

"'Dear John' (the band's first single) stood out, although a couple of tracks do require a twin guitar (notably 'May The Sunshine,' although the vocals did handle this well, and the acoustic guitar was good), and it would be nice to have a little more 1980s and 1990s included.

"Despite the temperature-induced thinning of the crowd, the set finished with energy and pace (if slightly predictably track-wise).

"After the show, the band talked to fans, and Rodney Matthews seemed under the cosh, too. Lovely to meet so many fans from around the world (I didn't have time to chat to all), although the number of (quite clearly) non-Celts wearing kilts did seem odd.

"The end of an era of one of Britain's best, most successful, and hardest-working classic rock bands and the start of their next era with a well-organized (ahem, the cost of the drinks) fan-oriented event. The resultant DVD should be good.

Set list

1 — "Silver Dollar Forger"
2 — "Sleeptalker"
3 — "When The Light Comes Down"
4 — "Rock 'n' Roll Telephone"
5 — "Razamanaz"
6 — "Miss Misery"

7 – "May the Sunshine"
8 – "See Me"
9 – "Dear John"
10 – "Turn On Your Receiver"
11 – "Radio"
12 – "Bad Bad Boy"
13 – "Shanghai'd in Shanghai"
14 – "Heart's Grown Cold"
15 – "Holiday"
16 – "One Set Of Bones/This Flight Tonight"
17 – "Broken Down Angel"

Encore

1 – "Hair of the Dog"
2 – "Love Hurts"
3 – "Expect No Mercy"

Michael Tasker's account: "About 120 of us were packed into a tiny studio to be part of the recording. It was hot and loud, and the band did the best they could in trying circumstances. For many, it was the first time we had seen Linton, and there was a little apprehension amongst the regular faces that seem to congregate at events likes these. Just what would the band sound like? What would be the dynamics? The vibe?

The performance did not quite fill us with much confidence for the future.

"On a brighter note, it was the first time most had heard 'Dear John' played live, a lovely, little belter of a number. And the legend that is Rodney Mathews was in attendance and exhibited his artwork."

On November 20, Nazareth played a show in Ekaterinburg, Russia, where Osborne tells the audience that "Dan McCafferty says, 'hello,'" getting the expected cheer from the crowd.

At that point in the tour, and without knowing what may be going on behind the scenes, the band seems to be struggling a bit. They get lost for a moment at the beginning of "Beggar's Day" (something for which Osborne can't be held responsible), and a sluggish "Hair of the Dog" plods forward like never before. At least the addition of "Animals" from 1989's *Snakes 'n' Ladders* as the encore is a surprising, if curious, choice.

On November 28, at the Theatre Du Palace in Bienne, Switzerland, the set list received some fine tuning. The addition of "Silver Dollar Forger" and the live debut of "Sleeptalker" (from 2011's *Big Dogz*) were welcomed, and the version of "When The Lights Come Down" was surprisingly well done.

The band ended the year with a series of concerts cancelled due to Linton reportedly having issues with his throat.

In January of 2015, Linton made the following statement on his personal Facebook page:

> Official Announcement: I am no longer a member of Nazareth. It didn't work out, for me, or for the band. I'd like to thank Pete, Jimmy & Lee for the opportunity. I'd also like to thank Dan for his support and encouragement. Most of all, I'd like to thank the fans—you guys are something else, and because of you it has all been worthwhile. I hope to see you all again in the future at one of my own gigs. I'd also like to wish my successor all the best and Nazareth a fantastic 2015 and beyond.
>
> Linton

Manny Charlton
1990–2015

After leaving Nazareth in 1990, original guitarist Manny Charlton kept busy with a variety of projects, although none of them reached the peaks of his former occupation. Actually, while still in the band, Charlton was enlisted to handle production duties in 1986 for the up and coming band Guns N' Roses. Unfortunately, after recording "Paradise City," two versions of "Move to the City," "November Rain," "Shadow of your Love" (takes one and two), and "Reckless Life," Charlton had to abandon the project in order to continue Nazareth duties. The material was re-recorded for the release of the 1987 multi-platinum *Appetite For Destruction* album, in which Charlton receives thanks in the credits.

Charlton's debut solo album, *Drool*, was released in 1999. Although heavy in parts, it is dragged down by the generic "rock dude" lead vocals that Neil Miller provides. The record has a bar band version of Neil Young's "Rockin' In The Free World" that adds nothing to the original.

In fact, some subtraction may have occurred. More interesting is a batch of rerecorded Nazareth songs. "Donna—Get Off That Crack" has unfortunate 1980s hair metal vocals. "White Boy" and "Animals" are surprising choices, and Charlton's still authoritative slide guitar intro to "Lady Luck" is encouraging, as is the grinding groove his backing musicians buttress beneath him. Unfortunately, Miller doesn't have the required authority to bring things home. However, one has to admire the level of confidence Charlton has to give space on his initial release for songs from Nazareth's 1986 effort *Cinema* and the not exactly classic 1989 album *Snakes 'n' Ladders*.

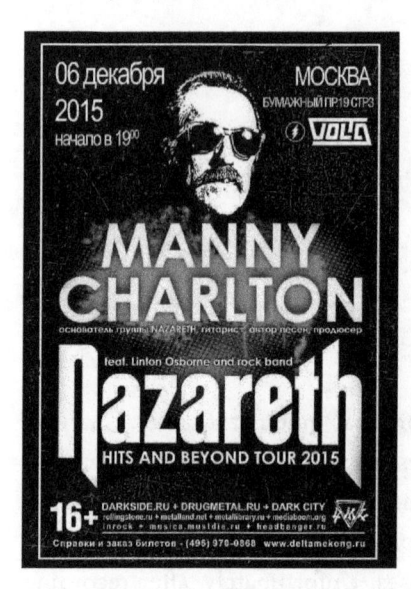

In 2000, Charlton released *Bravado*, a bold title to be sure. The album kicks off with a cover of the *Cinema* track "Hit The Fan," delivered with flat vocals and tinny drums but a pretty propulsive rhythm. Again, Charlton's choice of Nazareth tunes to revisit is commendable, showing the guitarist's faith in the quality of the material and perhaps his desire to give these tracks another shot at public acceptance. As for the other songs, the guitar solo in "The Difference" is flown in on top of the track with a completely different texture, to its detriment, and on "Legends," Charlton's vocals sound amazingly like post-Pink Floyd Roger Waters. It's not necessarily a bad thing, but it is perhaps a bit odd, as this is the only time this occurs.

Bravado ends with a raw demo take of "One From The Heart," another song from the 1986 *Cinema* album.

Next up for Charlton was 2001's *Stonkin'* (credited to the Manny Charlton Band), a heavy-handed "rawk" record bordering at times on grunge. This release is comprised solely of original material, which may or may not be a good thing depending on your philosophical bent. The track "Not Disappearing" is noteworthy for some evocative soloing from Charlton, some of his best playing since leaving Nazareth.

In 2002, Charlton reissued *Raz Em Alive*, the limited "official" bootleg of Nazareth's tremendous July 22, 1989 show in Illertissen, Germany on the *Snakes 'n' Ladders* tour.

Klone This (2003), credited to the Manny Charlton Band, features Steve Vinson on lead vocals and benefits from having an actual band playing real instruments, which seems to have invigorated Charlton, who offers some memorably tasty riffs throughout. *Klone This* is comprised completely of original material with no Nazareth songs included. The final track, "A Ballad For Karin & Astrid," contains some expressive and sensitive playing from Charlton.

Say The Word (2004) is stripped down musically compared to earlier efforts and has Charlton handling all of the lead vocals. The first Nazareth cover, "This Month's Messiah," has some interesting instrumental areas (including backwards guitar), and you can't fault the choice of material, but the drums sound like wet cardboard, and the vocals can't come anywhere near McCafferty's epic roar. Curiously, Charlton also covers the more recent Naz track (and one he had no hand in writing) "Walk By Yourself," with surprising results. By slowing down the arrangement and using a Bob Geldof-style vocal, Charlton makes the tune his own, which is commendable. It helps that the original song is such a strong piece of songwriting. "Where I Live" is an interesting pastiche of Beatles-inspired psychedelic moves, while Dylan's "Boots Of Spanish Leather" (which McCafferty covered on his 1975 self-titled solo album) relies heavily on the echo effect but is vindicated by lovely complementary acoustic and electric guitar parts.

Fans who ordered *Say The Word* directly from Charlton could also purchase the bonus Nazareth disc *The Garage Tapes Vol. 1*, a homemade-looking CD-R of four rare, previously unreleased tracks. "Body Heat" is a demo for 1986's *Cinema* album and boasts a driving arrangement and slashing guitar moves. The 1989 *Snakes 'n' Ladders* demo for "See You, See Me" was released officially on the 2011 4 CD set *The Naz Box*, as were exclusives from Charlton's CD-R. "Child In The Sun" is listed as being a "ruff mix" of the *Loud 'n' Proud* (1973) track, but the hollow-sounding drums, unlike on the album version, suggest this is a demo as well. Finally, the excellent instrumental "Snaefell," featuring Zal Cleminson, was be released as a bonus track on the 2010 Salvo reissue of 1979's *No Mean City* album.

A collaboration with drummer Steve Froese (meaning that Charlton plays all other instruments), *Sharp* (2004) is an unfussy collection of cover songs suffering from thin production values (Where on Earth did they record the drums?) and even thinner lead vocals.

Tracks include Elvis Presley's "My Baby Left Me" and "Blue Moon Of Kentucky," a radically re-arranged take on Bob Dylan's "All Along The Watchtower," Emmylou Harris's "Deeper Well," and a sensitive reading of "Shelter From The Storm" (Dylan again). Charlton also revisits his Nazareth years with new renditions of Tim Hardin's "Hang On To A Dream" (from *Snakes 'n' Ladders*) and "Please Don't Judas Me" (*Hair of the Dog*) with added backwards guitar playing. Also included are a couple of instrumental originals, which, frankly, is an area worth pursuing for the guitarist.

For an extra five dollars,, fans who ordered *Sharp* could also get another CD-R of four rare Nazareth cuts, *The Garage Tapes Vol. 2*. This "release" kicks off with an extremely valuable early demo of the *Malice In Wonderland* (1980) track "Big Boy" featuring Zal Cleminson, pristine vocal harmonies, and fun Darrel Sweet hand-slap percussion. The next three tracks were released on Nazareth's 2011 *The Naz Box* set, "SOS" (*Sound Elixir* outtake), "Mexico" (*2XS* demo) and "Sunshine Of Your Love" (*Snakes 'n' Ladders* outtake).

In 2005, Charlton released *Sharp Re-Loaded* with more covers like Fleetwood Mac's "The Chain," an interesting take on the Byrds' "So You Want To Be A Rock 'n' Roll Star," The Beatles' "Norwegian Wood," and Bob Dylan's "Wicked Messenger," among others. Again, the Nazareth years were represented with a noisy "Cinema" (an inspired choice for sure, from the 1986 album of the same name) and "Fallen Angel," from 1980's *Malice In Wonderland*, with vocals from Swedish singer Emil Gammeltoft.

A double-CD reissue from Angel Air in 2014 combined *Sharp* with *Sharp Re-Loaded* and added two bonus tracks to each.

A short-lived collaboration with ex-Samson vocalist Nicky Moore under the band name From Behind resulted in the 2006 album *Game Over* that finally challenged Charlton with a powerhouse voice. The failure of From Behind to reach its full potential remains an unfortunate part of the Manny Charlton story.

Americana Deluxe (2007) includes the Nazareth songs "Salty Salty" from 1986's *Cinema* and the *Expect No Mercy* outtake "Desolation Road," both rendered respectfully although not really noteworthy. More interesting is the track "Danko/Manuel," a fitting tribute to the two deceased members of the Band, Rick Danko and Richard Manuel.

Then There's This (2008) has Manny's take on "New York Broken Toy," originally from *Expect No Mercy* (1977), and a cover of "The Letter," a number one hit for the Box Tops in 1967.

Also in 2008, Charlton formed a new band that toured under the unfortunate name "Nazareth Featuring Manny Charlton." This tactical misstep caused much confusion for fans who attended shows not knowing that Charlton would be the only recognizable face onstage. After legal notification from the real Nazareth, Charlton changed the name of his group.

Hellacious (2013) has lead vocals from newcomer Robin DeLorenzo for an unfortunate mix of grunge and nu metal, including a re-recording of "Family" from *Drool* (1999). An acoustic cover of Nazareth's "Heart's Grown Cold" has a slight country lilt to it, which is decent enough and a welcome respite from the rest of the overly aggressive album. Another Naz cover, "Changin' Times" (from 1975's *Hair of the Dog*) is given a pretty faithful reading. *Hellacious* also has contributions from Irish guitarist Vivian Campbell (Dio, Def Leppard), drummer Steven Adler (Guns N' Roses), and bassist Tim Bogert (Vanilla Fudge, Cactus, Beck Bogert & Appice). Charlton returned the favour to DeLorenzo by appearing on her 2014 solo album *Walkin' Miles In My Shoes*.

The fact that Charlton has re-recorded over fifteen different Nazareth songs from his past, one wonders if a compilation of these retakes has been considered. It sure seems like a viable and possibly lucrative option. Having all these re-recordings in one place certainly would be attractive to hardcore Nazareth fans who have lost track of what Scotland's original guitar hero has been up to.

European blues band the Fluffy Jackets recruited Charlton to attend recording sessions at Sun Studios in Memphis in October 2011. The resulting album, *Fighting Demons*, was released in 2014 and has Charlton laying down melodic and lyrical solos over the band's original material, to great effect. Simply put, this record has some of Charlton's most zestful playing in years.

In 2014, Charlton joined Spanish metal band Sacramento for a mini-tour in their home country (and Charlton's birthplace). The tour touched down in Villana, Alicante (August 8), Martos, Jaen (August 9) and Estepona, Malaga (August 10), with an eleven-song set list including classics from the guitarist's back catalogue, such as "Boys In The Band," "Miss Misery," "Dream On," "Back to the Trenches," "Expect No Mercy," "Razamanaz," and "Hair of the Dog."

In October 2015, Charlton appeared for two shows (October 16 and 17) with the band Estirpe in Cordoba, Spain , where he played "Hair of the Dog" and Led Zeppelin's "Rock And Roll."

Later in 2015, Charlton shocked the Nazareth fan community with the announcement that he had formed a new band with estranged ex-Naz lead vocalist Linton Osborne. The group, known as Sonz Of Bitchez, posted two demo recordings on their new website as a taste of what the two were up to.

"All My Tears" is a cover of a Julie Miller track from her excellent 1999 album *Broken Things*. Osborne's vocals are swamped with echo, but he is singing in a bit of a lower range than he was in Nazareth, which is a good thing. Charlton provides a swirling guitar solo for the song. Regardless of what one thinks of the finished product, the lads get full respect for the choice of material they chose to cover.

The second song Sonz Of Bitches posted was "Xpect No Mercy," a slightly retitled cover of the 1977 Nazareth cut "Expect No Mercy." The track benefits from full-frontal guitars, but the programmed percussion fails where real flesh and blood drums are required. Osborne's vocals have a distortion effect on them, which is a bit interesting at least. The recording of these two songs was a long-distance operation, with each of the musicians laying down their parts in Scotland and Spain, respectively.

Before Sonz Of Bitchez even played their first show, the name had been changed to the Manny Charlton Band Featuring Linton Osborne. The new band made their live debut during a warm-up gig on December 3, 2015 at Backstage At the Green, an intimate music venue with a capacity of 120 located in the Green Hotel in Kinross, Perthshire, Scotland.

The show opened with "This Month's Messiah" and surprisingly included "Donna Get Off That Crack" (from *Snakes 'n' Ladders*), leading directly into the instrumental "Rose In The Heather" (from *Hair of the Dog*), which, to date, Nazareth has never performed live.

The next night of the tour, December 5, saw the band playing Ben Club Hall in Ekaterinburg, Russia. This show consisted of the same set list, although it omitted "Woke Up This Morning."

The final gig of the brief mini-tour took place on December 6 at Club Volta in Moscow. It had a decent light show, giving the band a more professional appearance than seen at the Scotland gig.

Again, the band played a selection of Nazareth tunes plus "Family" and "Sleep" from Charlton's 1999 *Drool* album. A highlight of the tour is a bleak cover of Julie Miller's "All My Tears" from the band's original demo. The rarity "Rose in the Heather" spotlighted some wonderfully emotive and expressive soloing from the guitarist. Sporting an AC/DC *Back In Black* T-shirt, Osborne introduced the final song with the poignant observation, "Things are always changing," before the band burrowed deep into the groove of "Changin' Times." The young musicians thrust the beat forward during the coda for more high-wattage soloing from Charlton. The encore of "Woke Up This Morning" begins with frenetic slide guitar playing from the legendary axe-slinger.

With the tour over, the band retreated to their respective homelands with the promise of more dates to come in 2016.

Carl Sentence and No Means Of Escape
2015

Without much of a mention about the Osborne situation, in February, Welsh vocalist Carl Sentance was named as the new Nazareth frontman. Sentance is a journeyman metal singer who has performed with Persian Risk, Tokyo Blade, the Geezer Butler Band, Krokus, and Deep Purple keyboardist Don Airey's solo band. Sentance also released a solo album in 2008 called *Mind Doctor*, which had the vocalist channeling his inner Bon Scott (not a bad thing) on some songs that veer a bit too close to Bon-era AC/DC (not a good thing). The chorus to "Girl's Got Fire" is a virtual rewrite of "Girls Got Rhythm." Similarly, the track "Old School" sits uncomfortably close to "Rock 'n' Roll Damnation."

Although never linked to any single, massively successful project, Sentance has logged enough miles on the unforgiving road to rock to be able to deliver the goods professionally, if not with a sense of hard rock flair. He also brings a subtle instrumental addition to the band, playing tambourine occasionally, something neither of his predecessors had done.

Sentance made his live debut with the band at a show in Hameenlinna, Finland on April 17, 2015 performing a set that balanced classics ("Dream On" and "This Flight Tonight") with deep cuts ("Silver Dollar Forger" and "Turn On Your Receiver") and newer material ("One Set Of Bones" and "Rock 'n' Roll Telephone"). The new lineup encored with the crowd favorites "Love Hurts" and "Morning Dew."

Touring throughout Europe brought the group to Breslau, Poland on May 1, where they played crunching versions of "Expect No Mercy" and "Hair of the Dog," among others.

On May 20, McCafferty performed "Love Hurts" and "We Are Animals" with the Luigi Sferrazza Orchestra in Sochi, Russia.

A show entitled "The Legends of Rock" at East End Park in Dunfermline, Scotland on May 30 featured opening acts Stevie Agnew and Hurricane Road and then Big Country followed by Nazareth. The band delivered a blue-collar rendition of "Morning Dew" with Sentance beginning in a lower register that made the eventual liftoff that much more impactful.

A momentous highlight of the year occurred when, incredibly, for the encore of "Broken Down Angel," McCafferty took to the stage for lead vocal duties. Sentance respectfully relegated himself to providing backing vocals for this historic moment, which also had the poignant sight of McCafferty singing the chorus with his arm around his old lieutenant, Pete Agnew.

An intimate Nazareth club show in Hanover, Germany on October 26 had the expected hits ("Razamanaz," "Hair of the Dog," and "Expect No Mercy") but also a decent run-through of "Miss Misery," "One Set Of Bones," and "Changing Times."

In October, the London show from November 14, 2014 was released on DVD and Blu-ray. Titled *No Means Of Escape*, (with new *No Mean*

City-inspired artwork courtesy of Rodney Matthews), this was Linton Osborne's swan song with the band.

The show itself opens with a strong version of "Silver Dollar Forger," although Osborne's yelp leans a little too hard on the last word in the line "I want to walk out in the sun!"

Next up, "Sleeptalker" (from 2011's *Big Dogz*) leads right into "Rock 'n' Roll Telephone," which is interesting, but the vocals during "May The Sunshine" are unnecessarily harsh. A muscular "One Set Of Bones" goes straight into "This Flight Tonight," another decent move, but "Hair of the Dog" plods musically. Overall, the concert never really jells into a solid performance. The band sounds tentative, and Osborne is an awkward fit at best. The "linebacker among hobbits'" physical presence doesn't help either.

This concert was only released after Murrison and Agnew spent time in the studio redoing much of their respective parts and adjusting the track listing. "When The Light Comes Down," "Dear John," "Radio," "Shanghai'd In Shanghai," "Heart's Grown Cold," "Holiday," and "Broken Down Angel" were all performed at the concert but were edited out of the home video. It is especially disappointing that some interesting song choices were removed from the finished product Luckily, bonus material on the disc adds some much-needed extra value. A duo reading of "Sunshine" between Osborne and Jimmy Murrison playing a twelve-string acoustic guitar is fine. Osborne handles himself better with low-key performances like this.

"Made In Scotland" is an engaging, fifty-minute documentary tracing different aspects of the band's history, although it's a little odd that the stories are presented not quite chronologically. *No Mean City* cover artist Rodney Matthews is included among the interviewees. An excellent supplemental feature, "Meet the Super Fans," is a thirteen-minute piece interviewing many of the supporters who came to the show (a few of whom contributed to this book).

Bonus interviews with Pete Agnew and Dan McCafferty are actually just unedited footage from the "Made In Scotland" documentary.

The *No Means Of Escape* cover artwork is a lost opportunity, being just a re-hash of the classic *No Mean City* imagery. A more original concept would have been to have Fred doing something different, not just posing the same way to cash in on the previous artwork's success. It's like a cover song that doesn't really add anything new to the original. This is opposite of the way Nazareth does things usually.

While it's good that the band has finally approved a Blu-ray release, a lot more could have been done with the format. I hope some vintage McCafferty shows will be considered even if shot in standard definition. Numerous bands have had a steady stream of quality home video releases. Naz fans deserve a few as well.

Also in 2015, McCafferty appeared on the debut album *First Wave* by ex-Yngwie Malmsteen sidemen Michael Vescera and Barry Sparks recording under the band name Riot On Mars. Covering Nazareth's version of "Beggar's Day" from 1975's *Hair of the Dog* album, McCafferty supplies gritty co-lead vocals. Riot On Mars even goes so far as to include the "Rose In The Heather" coda to the song, as heard on the original record.

Nazareth ended the year with the encouraging announcement that in 2016, there would be additional tour dates with Carl Sentance's skillful wail powering the sonic engine.

CPSIA information can be obtained
at www.ICGtesting.com
Printed in the USA
BVHW08s1502150618
519069BV00002B/51/P

9 781460 286395